Physical Characteristics
Bull Terrier

(from the American Kennel Club bree⟨

Body: Well rounded with marked spring of rib, the back should be short and strong. The back ribs deep. The shoulders should be strong and muscular but without heaviness.

Tail: Short, set on low, fine, and ideally should be carried horizontally.

Coat: Short, flat, harsh to the touch and with a fine gloss.

Color: White: White though markings on the head are permissible. Colored: Any color other than white, or any color with white markings.

Underline: From the brisket to the belly should form a graceful upward curve.

Feet: Round and compact with well-arched toes like a cat.

Bull Terrier

◇

By Bethany Gibson

Contents

Training Your Bull Terrier   86

Begin with the basics of training the puppy and adult dog. Learn the principles of house-training the Bull Terrier, including the use of crates and basic scent instincts. Get started by introducing the pup to his collar and leash and progress to the basic commands. Find out about obedience classes and other activities.

Healthcare of Your Bull Terrier   113

By Lowell Ackerman DVM, DACVD
Become your dog's healthcare advocate and a well-educated canine keeper. Select a skilled and able veterinarian. Discuss breed-specific health concerns as well as pet insurance, vaccinations and infectious diseases, the neuter/spay decision and a sensible, effective plan for parasite control, including fleas, ticks and worms.

Showing Your Bull Terrier   146

Step into the center ring and find out about the world of the pure-bred dog sport. Here's how to get started in AKC conformation shows, how they are organized and what's required for your dog to become a champion. Take a leap into the realms of obedience trials, agility trials and tracking tests.

KENNEL CLUB BOOKS: **BULL TERRIER**
ISBN 13: 978-159378-229-0

Copyright © 2005, **2009** • Kennel Club Books® A Division of BowTie, Inc.
40 Broad Street, Freehold, New Jersey 07728 USA
Cover Design Patented: US 6,435,559 B2 • Printed in South Korea

Photography by

Paulette Braun, T.J. Calhoun, Carolina Biological Supply, David Dalton, Kent & Donna Dannen, Will de Veer, Isabelle Français, Carol Ann Johnson, Bill Jonas, Dr. Dennis Kunkel, Tam C. Nguyen, Antonio Philippe, Phototake, Jean Claude Revy, Alice Roche, Karen Taylor and Alice van Kempen.

Illustrations by:
Renée Low and Patricia Peters.

HISTORY OF THE
BULL TERRIER

Why the Bull Terrier was developed back in England in the 1800s has very little to do with today's Bull Terrier. The Bull Terrier is based on bull-and-terrier dogs, which were bred for baiting and dog fighting, sports that were eventually outlawed in Great Britain in the 19th century. These early dogs were bred for function, not form, and were completely devoted to their owners.

The origin of the Bull Terrier breed can be traced directly to a man named James Hinks, of Birmingham, England, who after years of experimentation introduced the breed in the 1850s. The Bull Terrier is based loosely on the now-extinct English White Terrier. Hinks spent years crossbreeding with bull-and-terrier dogs, attempting to build a bulldog that was not only better fitted to the pits but also better looking. By breeding out some traits seen in many early pit-fighting dogs, such as the roach back, overly angulated legs and undershot jaw, and injecting some size and strength (possibly from crossbreeding with the Spanish Pointer), the result was a handsome, proud gladiator, fit to walk next to a gentleman. The Bull Terrier retained a positive attribute of its

A Bull Terrier was the pet of the famed actress Miss Jean Melville. This photo was taken circa 1932.

OPPOSITE PAGE: The origin of the Bull Terrier, a breed established in the mid-1800s, was determined by the need of a single gentleman who desired a good-looking fighting dog. Enter our handsome gladiator, the Bull Terrier.

The extinct English White Terrier, an acknowledged forerunner of today's Bull Terrier. Photograph by C. Reid, circa 1890.

bull-and-terrier predecessors—unmatched loyalty to his owner.

If there was any question that the Bull Terrier was "too pretty" for the dog pits, the myth was quickly dispelled. The feisty, fight-to-the-death spirit of the Bull Terrier made him a relentless fighter in the pits, often beating dogs almost twice his size. Legend has it that Hinks himself once matched his 40-lb bitch Puss of Brum against the never-wary Mr. Tupper's 60-lb bull-and-terrier cross. Not only did "Puss" emerge victorious from the bloody bout, but Hinks whisked her away to the Holborn dog show later in the day—where she won a red ribbon!

The Bull Terrier was also quite a rat fighter, another unusual blood sport that was quite popular in England. Bull

Terriers held the unofficial records for most rats killed in minutes, hours and other time frames.

Though Hinks was quite proud of his creation's success in the dog- and rat-fighting pits, he was more interested in winning at the dog shows, which were beginning to rival dog fighting in popularity in Britain. In the 1860s, dog fanciers and show judges became partial to the all-white Bull Terriers; as a result, Hinks set forth to create a more consistently all-white breed. By culling piebald and brindle pups, breeding white dogs to white bitches and possibly introducing Dalmatian blood, Hinks was successful in creating all-white Bull Terriers. To this day, however, both types remain, classified as two varieties of the same breed, White and Colored Bull Terriers in the US and as one breed in the UK.

Throughout England, it became fashionable for gentlemen to sport Bull Terriers at their sides. Fearless, strong, loyal, well-mannered and friendly, the Bull Terrier was a stylish addition to the gentleman's retinue and became known as the "White Cavalier." The Bull Terrier's acceptance in upper-class society and success in the dog-show circuit were blessings, as the breed became known more as a people's dog than a fighting dog, eventually resulting in the friendly and typically peaceful Bull Terrier we know today.

WHITE CAVALIERS INVADE AMERICA
By David Harris

With the burgeoning popularity in Britain of James Hinks's new all-white Bull Terriers during the 1860s, it was inevitable that these so-called "White Cavaliers" would soon appear in America. The first such imports—Corvina and Puss III—are believed to have been brought back in 1869 by James Cruikshank of Pittsburgh. By 1877, when the Westminster Kennel Club staged its first "Bench Show of Dogs," 11 Bull Terriers were entered with names typical of the day like Nell, Rose, Jim, Billy and Lillie. Most were entered for sale, a common practice at early shows, with prices ranging from $50 to $500. The following year a show in Boston attracted no less than 23 Bull Terriers. James Watson noted that the first White Cavaliers of class shown in America were Ch. Tarquin—then the top winner in England—and his son Superbus, which were sent over in 1880 by Sir William Verner for exhibition in New York. The American Kennel Club (AKC) was established in Philadelphia in 1884, the first Bullterrier (AKC used one word rather than two until 1937) being entered in the stud book a year later. The entry reads "Nellie II, #3304. No sire or dam given . . ." Quite remarkably, however, Nellie II was one of the old-style brindles not a White Cavalier.

The most prominent figure in the breed at that time was Frank Dole of Connecticut, who imported, bred and sold numerous Bull Terriers. Many of his imports came from James Hinks's son Fred. Dole's biggest winner was Ch. Starlight, a daughter of the imports Ch. Grand Duke and the

From 1907, this Bull Terrier bitch, known as Millstone Venus, exhibits the changing fashion in breed type. She is much slighter and higher on leg, with a longer, nearly elegant neck.

great Ch. Maggie May. In 1899, at nearly 12 years old and with few front teeth left, the incredible Starlight was still able to win at a New York show. Two other stalwarts, William Faversham, the celebrated actor, and T.S. Bellin, did much to support and popularize the breed. Both were Englishmen who emigrated during the 1880s. The Bull Terrier Club of America (BTCA) was established initially, under the presidency of Frank Dole, in 1895. This was the year in which ear cropping was banned in Britain, a major blow to cropped breeds like Bull Terriers. And such was the belligerency of the new club on this matter that it was expelled from AKC membership for "conduct prejudicial to the welfare of the American Kennel Club." But by 1897 the BTCA was again a member club. In those days most members of the club's committee lived in New York, Connecticut and Massachusetts.

During the early 1890s Ch. Streatham Monarch and Ch. Carney, both English imports, battled for top honors. At a show in Chicago, judge Harry Goodman exercised the novel option of placing them "equal firsts". Goodman also judged the breed at the first Continental Kennel Club show in Denver in 1889. The BTCA held its inaugural show in New York in 1898, offering classes

BTCA

The Bull Terrier Club of America is the AKC parent club for the breed. The club's main purpose is to promote the Bull Terrier and protect the breed's best interests through club activities. The club provides owners, breeders and fanciers with a network of contacts in the US and also reaches out to Bull Terrier people all over the world. The club offers continuing education to those in the breed, as well as informing newcomers to the breed and helping them decide if the "Bully" is the breed for them. Their breeder referral service ensures new owners that they will be matched up with a reputable, ethical, knowledgeable breeder from which to obtain a puppy. The club has many regional affiliates and sanctions shows throughout the country. The major Bull Terrier event of the year is the BTCA's annual national specialty show. In addition, the club offers special awards and recognition to those dogs who've achieved success in the show ring and performance events. The BTCA's health committee supports research, studies and dissemination of information about health problems with the goal of eventually eliminating these problems from the Bull Terrier through careful breeding. The club also supports breed rescue, in which dedicated volunteers across the country take in Bullies from unfortunate situations, such as neglectful homes or animal shelters, caring for the dogs until they are placed in good homes. Visit the BTCA online at www.btca.com to acquaint yourself with all that the club does for the breed.

Ch. Haymarket Faultless, the winner of the 1918 Westminster show, was a milestone dog in America. From American parentage, Faultless was owned by Humphrey Elliott of Canada. American Bull Terriers had broader chests, were lower to the ground and their heads showed no stop but suggested a gentle arc.

for Bull Terriers over and under 30 pounds. The winner came down to a titanic struggle between "the three bright stars of the Bull Terrier firmament," namely Ch. Princeton Monarch, Ch. Tommy Tickle and Ch. Woodcote Wonder. The first two were bred by Bellin, while Dole owned the imported Woodcote Wonder. The judge, having placed Monarch first, took a leaf out of Goodman's book by giving Tickle and Wonder "equal seconds."

The ban on cropping had been a major setback for the breed in Britain. Meanwhile in America, where cropping was still allowed, the breed went from strength to strength: Bull Terrier entries at Westminster of 99 in 1901, 125 in 1902 and 147 in 1904. This last entry was adjudicated by a leading British judge, who was much impressed by the quality of the dogs in comparison to those back home. Woodcote Wonder, who had finally begun to establish supremacy over his rivals, was sent to California for a couple of years, indicating the breed was gaining a foothold there.

The year 1908 saw Noross Patrician gain his championship. Bred and owned by Dr. Alan Northridge of New York, Patrician "became the outstanding dog of the breed and his progeny carried his lines far and wide." In the midwest Ch. Bobby Buster, owned by Dwight Godard, of Aurora, Illinois, did wonders for the breed. While in San Francisco, E. Attridge bred several champions, his best being Ch. Edgecote Peer, who won the breed at Westminster in 1906, 1907 and again in 1908. Peer reputedly retired unbeaten. Next we come to Canadian Humphrey Elliott's

Ch. Furore Ferment, owned by Mr. and Mrs. Enno Meyer, epitomized the American-style Bull Terrier of the 1930s.

celebrated Ch. Haymarket Faultless. Although a Canadian dog, Faultless came out of American-bred parents, Noross Patrician and Glenmere Channel Queen. Billy Kendrick, a Bull Terrier stalwart and famous judge, provided a firsthand account of Faultless's unprecedented victory at Westminster in 1918. The two judges narrowed the field down to a top-winning Pekingese and Faultless, but couldn't agree on the winner. Kendrick wrote: ". . . hearts beat in unison with a single prayer on their lips when George S. Thomas was summoned as arbiter. Never was a Best in Show staged to quite so dramatic a tempo when Mr. Thomas, a truly great all-round personality, nodded in the direction of

Humphrey and Faultless. And then the crowd went wild. Never before was there a more popular Best in Show award." Faultless had become the first and only Bull Terrier to garner BIS at Westminster.

Almost inevitably the 1920s were something of a let-down, with neither the show entries nor the quality of new dogs matching up to those of the two earlier decades. Among the best of the new dogs was Ch. Coolridge Grit of Blight, imported by Wyatt Mayer of New York. Termed a "champion factory," Grit sired a record 14 American champions. By 1929 we saw the first champion with natural as opposed to cropped ears, namely Blodwen of Voewood. Ears continued as an issue with four states including New York prohibiting cropping. Then in 1931 the AKC ruled that cropped dogs could not be shown in states with cropping laws. And, though cropped ears were permitted in the breed standard until 1957, for all practical purposes the AKC's ruling meant that henceforth Bull Terriers were shown with natural ears.

By the 1930s American Bull Terriers—typically taller, narrower dogs with their brick-shaped heads—had diverged significantly in type from those preferred in Britain, which were lower stationed, cobbier and with the distinctly downfaced heads that are today a hallmark of the breed. A few enthusiasts, Bellin and Arthur Gale of Missouri among them, imported English dogs and were committed to propagating their type. But the majority of American breeders and especially of BTCA members focused their efforts on perfecting the type of Bull Terrier represented by Ch. Haymarket Faultless and the lines developed by Edmond Schmidt of Chicago (Artesian) and Frank Leach of Washington, D.C. (Newcoin). Ch. Furore Ferment, bred and owned by Enno Meyer of Ohio, is noted as a prime example of the type. But the imports were gaining ground with the 1933 show scene being dominated by the great English bitch Ch. Faultless of Blighty. She became the first and only Bull Terrier to win BIS at Montgomery County and went on to win the 1934 BTCA specialty. Later she was sold to film star Dolores Del Rio, reputedly for $5000.

Also out in California, Dr. George Lewin established his Kanyon kennels, with top imports as well as American-bred dogs. Without question, however, the top breeder-exhibitor of the 1930s was Mrs. Jessie Platt Bennett of Pennsylvania with her Coolyn Hill dogs. Having imported some beautifully bred stock, she went on to breed many

winners, among them Ch. Coolyn Quicksilver and the rest of the famous Silver litter, all of which became champions. The top winner from 1939-41 was her Ch. Coolyn North Wind. Then in 1940 Mrs. Bennett brought over the stellar Ch. Raydium Brigadier, the epitome of English type. The sire of a then record 17 champions, Brigadier sealed the fate of the American-style dogs, which simply disappeared from the scene.

The differences in type between English and American dogs may have resulted in heated discourse and some animosity, but this pales besides the dispute over Colored Bull Terriers that spanned the 1930s and 1940s. It was little short of all-out war and, had it taken place 50 years beforehand, we may well have

A champion in England and America, Ch. Raydium Brigadier represented the classic English type. He was imported by Mrs. Jessie Platt Bennett of Coolyn Hills kennels in Pennsylvania. Note the type differences between Brigadier and Furore Ferment.

been reviewing another gun fight at the O.K. Corral. Enthusiasts in England had begun to breed colored versions of the White Cavalier early in the century, such that the first colored champion was crowned in 1931. Then in 1934 Wallace Mollison of Massachusetts imported the first of these new "Coloreds"– Tisman's Tango and Brigadier of Blighty. He bred them and in 1935 Tango whelped the first litter of Coloreds bred in America. Coloreds first appeared at Westminster in 1936, when one took second place to a white bitch in the Open Class. The first colored champion, Mrs. Willard McCortney's Beltona Brindigal, completed her title the following year. The Bull Terrier establish-

ment was outraged by these events. The BTCA, under the presidency of Father Francis Heaney of Staten Island, viewed itself as the guardian of the all-white Bull Terrier and regarded the Coloreds literally as mongrels. Opposition took the form of verbal warfare and the boycotting of shows and judges who supported Coloreds. Father Heaney, it was said, was a saintly man: he would forgive anything except supporting the Coloreds.

The BTCA wanted Coloreds to be registered not as Bull Terriers, but as a separate breed. To this end, in 1936 the BTCA revised its standard to disqualify "markings behind the set on of head." The AKC, however, proved equal to the challenge by approving the new standard and then adopting a new one for the Coloreds as a separate variety of Bull Terrier with "Any color other than white, or any color with white markings. White not to predominate." The BTCA continued to wage war, but in 1942 the AKC resolved the issue, determining that Whites and Coloreds should be separate varieties of the same breed. Not until 1949 did the BTCA finally vote to accept this decision. The ultimate acceptance of Coloreds owes much to two men, namely Mollison and in particular Herbert Stewart of Pennsylvania. Of note here, America is the only country in which Whites and Coloreds are

Ch. Heir Apparent at Monty-Ayr, owned by Dr. and Mrs. E. S. Montgomery, was the first American-bred Bull Terrier to win an all-breed Best in Show, an accomplishment he made on August 13, 1946 at a dog show in Albion, Michigan.

classified as varieties of Bull Terriers rather than as just one breed.

Post World War II the leading figure in the breed was Dr. E. S. Montgomery of Pennsylvania, a giant of a man in all respects of the phrase. He purchased the bitch Tanark Queen Mother, bred from English lines by Willard McCortney of Michigan. Montgomery mated her to Raydium Brigadier, thereby producing Ch. Heir Apparent at Monty-Ayr, an all-breed BIS winner and the sire of a record 17 champions. At one show where Heir Apparent was competing for BIS, Dr. Montgomery, sensing the judge was equivocating, picked up the dog and threw him fully 6 feet with Heir Apparent landing perfectly. And Montgomery kept doing this until the judge awarded his dog BIS!

The 1950s and 1960s were dull years for the breed. Yes, Montgomery's Monty-Ayr dogs continued their winning ways and several imports pursued successful show careers. None of these dogs, however, made a lasting impact on the breed, and it became clear that American-bred Bull Terriers lacked the type and quality of their British counter-parts. Bill and Hope Colket of Pennsylvania (Silverwood kennels) determined to establish a trophy competition for North American-bred dogs, along the

lines of the English trophies, to be awarded by breeder-judges. With the encouragement of Raymond Oppenheimer, a great figure in the world of Bull Terriers, the Colkets set about the task. Tragically, however, both were killed in auto accidents and so the Silverwood Trophy became a memorial to them. A second initiative followed with the introduction of a Recognition of Merit (ROM) system, an award based on success at specialty and supported shows adjudicated by breeder-judges. These two initiatives have gone from strength to strength, truly transforming Bullterrierdom in America.

The first Silverwood Trophy, an unpretentious event held in 1970, went to Ch. Killer Joe, bred

The first Silverwood Trophy winner, this is Ch. Killer Joe, owned by Peggy Arnaud.

Ch. Jarrogue's Ms. Jennifer Jones, bred by George Schreiber and owner Susan C. Murphy.

1976 Silverwood winner, raised the stakes in terms of the international standing of North American dogs. They have consistently bred top winners, including Ch. Magor Moonshine, the 1996 Silverwood winner. A guiding figure throughout the Silverwood years has been and is Hon. David Merriam of California, past president of both the AKC and the BTCA.

In the east, Drue King (Westbrook) made excellent use of the line produced by her neighbor Peggy Arnaud with Ch. Westbrook Wild One and the brindle Westbrook Windborne, both winning the Silverwood Trophy in the early 1980s. On the other side of the country, Bob and Lynne Myall (Iceni) of Bothell, Washington imported the great Ch. Monkery Buckskin, a son of the famed English sire Ch. Souperlative Jackadandy of Ormandy. Buckskin soon garnered all of the breed's stud records, siring a multitude of winners. The Myalls have bred numerous top Bull Terriers, including their 1997 Silverwood winner Ch. Iceni Isis. David and Anna Harris of New Mexico arrived from England with a penchant for Coloreds and among the dogs they brought with them was the key Jackadandy daughter Ch. Jaquenetta of Brummagem, granddam of the brindle Ch. Brummagem Bacarole, a

and owned by Peggy Arnaud of Massachusetts. The following year the winner was Ch. Banbury Charity Buttercup, bred and owned by Winkie Mackay-Smith of Philadelphia and now Virginia, for whom this was the beginning of an illustrious career as a breeder, exhibitor and mentor. Her brindle Ch. Banbury Benson of Bedrock took the Terrier Group at Westminster in 1982 and became an influential sire (Bedrock here being the affix of her current partner Mary Remer of Pennsylvania). Another kennel that has exerted enormous influence during what we can call the Silverwood years is Magor, belonging to Norma and Gordon Smith of Thunder Bay in Canada. Their Ch. Magor the Marquis, the

Silverwood runner-up. George Schreiber (Zodiac kennels) of New Jersey exerted tremendous influence on the breed during the 1980s. Having bred the first Colored to win the Silverwood trophy, Ch. Ann-Dee's Red Adair in 1979, Schreiber mated his Ch. Zodiac Lady Madonna to the top import Ch. Catrana Eye Opener of Aricon, producing the key litter-mates Ch. Zodiac Jarrogue Prima Donna and Ch. Zodiac Private Eye, who between them produced the four Silverwood winners from 1988 to 1991.

The most successful kennels of the late 1980s and 1990s have been those of Dr. Franne Berez (Action) of Pittsburgh and Susan Murphy (Jarrogue) of Orange County, California, both having bred six and four Silverwood winners respectively. Ch. Jarrogue's Ms. Jennifer Jones and Ch. Action Hot Item won in 1988 and 1989 respectively. These two spectacular bitches are further proof that American-breds were a match for Bull Terriers anywhere in the world. Interestingly, although both these kennels' early successes were with White Bull Terriers, they have since had success with Coloreds, including Ch. Jarrogue's Red Rover in 1998 and Ch. Action African Queen in 2000.

Indeed, during the 1990s the Coloreds, for the first time, enjoyed consistently greater success than their White brethren. In the new century, Bill and Becky Poole's Rocky Top kennel in Tennessee has come to the fore with a number of imported and home-bred dogs. Their top winner is multiple specialty and BIS Ch. Rocky Top's Sundance Kid, whom the Pooles co-own with several others. Sundance Kid, the 2001 Silverwood winner, was sired by the topnotch German dog Ch. Einstein the Joker, indicating the international flavor of Bullterrierdom today. American Bull Terriers have made tremendous advances in the past twenty or so years, with superior examples of both White and Colored varieties winning in the all-breed as well as their own specialty shows. Truly, the White Cavalier and his Colored brother have invaded and conquered America.

Ch. Action Hot Item, the 1989 Silverwood Trophy winner, bred by Rich and Maureen Ciecwisz and owner Dr. Franne Berez.

Bull Terriers are very popular around the world, as this Dutch beauty signifies. This bitch is a Dutch champion and multiple Group winner.

CHARACTERISTICS OF THE
BULL TERRIER

Do you want a Bull Terrier? Do you want a dog that is playful, active, curious, quirky, clownish, sensitive, loyal, affectionate and attached to his owner(s)? Before you scream out "yes!", you must further consider these things: do you want a dog that is stubborn, willful, overconfident, aggressive, bossy, dominant and destructive? Now you're not so sure? Then read on...

PERSONALITY

The Bull Terrier certainly is not the dog for everyone, but those who reluctantly accept the Bull Terrier's drawbacks are paid back in spades for the breed's positive traits. The Bull Terrier personality is undoubtedly the greatest trait of this unique dog. Undying devotion and loyalty to his family are coupled with clownish curiosity and playfulness to make

Bull Terrier cousins include the Miniature Bull Terrier (two dogs in center) and the American Staffordshire Terrier (on either end). All bull-and-terrier breeds share certain characteristics.

the Bully a lifelong friend that is an absolute joy to own and watch. The Bull Terrier is entertaining as he investigates new surroundings with the unending enthusiasm of a child and the tenacious attention to detail of a crime-scene investigator. When introduced to an object of any kind—be it a stuffed animal, a tennis ball or you name it—the Bull Terrier will inspect it, play with it and eventually try to either eat it or destroy it. This makes for great entertainment on a lazy Sunday afternoon.

Without objects to play with, the Bull Terrier is certainly creative enough to keep himself occupied. (Owners quickly learn that it is far more astute to provide appropriate toys than to lose valuable possessions.) In fact, the unending desire to keep busy is a typical trait—something quite common among all puppies but a lifetime characteristic for the Bull Terrier. Your Bull Terrier will find something to do; if you are present, his job is to make you laugh. He's something of an exhibitionist, so don't be surprised to see your Bull Terrier showing off his athleticism by sprinting back and forth across the room, jumping or attacking inanimate objects—all in the name of keeping your attention. Should you get involved in playtime with him, you will not be disappointed. Toss a ball and watch your Bull Terrier pursue it with persistent vigor—leaping over and running through everything in his way with a speed that will both impress and delight you.

The big bull couldn't bully the Bull Terrier. It takes no small amount of courage to stand up to an animal 20 times your size!

During a rousing romp on the beach, this Bull Terrier has no problem keeping up with his giant Great Pyrenees chum. All dogs play with their mouths open, but they learn how to play-bite so that their playmates aren't injured.

Have you ever heard the saying, "He'd run into a brick wall for you?" It was probably started by the owner of a Bull Terrier, as these dogs seem to enjoy ramming headfirst into solid objects. In fact, it is not unusual for a Bull Terrier to race about the house, bumping his head against the walls and furniture, as an expression of his desire to play with you. As alarming as you may find this performance, it will be hard for you to stay indifferent—you will soon find yourself laughing and eventually playing with your crazy Bull Terrier.

If his athletic prowess does not grab your attention, then you

Though not regarded as a bird dog, the Bull Terrier is curious enough to inspect this feathery carcass.

As terriers, or "earth dogs," Bull Terriers have been used to rid the landscape of vermin. The breed's ratting instinct is frequently tested during special events like this one that took place in Colorado.

The Bull Terrier is not really an all-weather dog. Snow is a novelty, but after a short time outdoors in cold (or heat) he will prefer the comforts of the indoors.

may want to close your ears. Believe it or not, your Bull Terrier may soon be asking for you. That's right, many Bull Terriers can "talk!" They can't recite Shakespearean verses, but they will grunt, groan and grumble. These amusing vocalizations are not to be confused with growling (which the Bull Terrier will do when necessary). The Bull Terrier makes great attempts at conversation and you will learn to interpret his various noises. Once provided with some kind of reaction, he will use his seemingly unlimited vocabulary on a regular basis. This endearing trait may be annoying or strange to some people, but Bull Terrier owners thoroughly enjoy and revel in it.

You've probably guessed by now that the Bull Terrier desperately craves and needs human attention. Bull Terriers are very family-oriented and are not happy when kept apart from the family.

You will need to accept your Bull Terrier as a member of the family and include him in family activities and excursions. If you cannot take your Bull Terrier with you on an extended trip, by all means find someone to watch him. It does not take much time for the Bull Terrier to get lonely and depressed. Luckily, this breed is very sociable and will quickly accept someone introduced as a friend.

Look at your Bull Terrier and you will be returned a loving gaze from coal-black eyes. These same eyes will glint when he knows he's being naughty, but will love you just as much and expect the same in return. In fact, he loves you so much it may drive you mad, as it is not uncommon for a Bull Terrier literally to sit on top of you—be it at your feet, on your lap or anywhere else you'll allow him—every moment of the day! Bull Terriers do not sit near you; they sit *on* you. Hopefully you'll find this intimacy endearing, for it

This young lady has become an honorary part of a Bully puppy pack. Few breeds are as fun-loving and comical as the Bull Terrier.

is more than difficult to get him to move once he's settled down on a warm, cozy part of your body. A true Bull Terrier is a most stubborn animal; you'd have more luck moving a mule than a Bull Terrier.

Perhaps that's where the breed's name comes from: their rather bullish obstinacy. Your Bull Terrier is occupying your favorite chair? Make life easy on yourself and find a new favorite chair for the moment. Don't be surprised, either, when he makes a move as if he wants to go out to do his business, then jumps in your warm chair the minute you get up to open the door! Overbearing? Yes. Obstinate? Yes. Neurotic? Well, for a dog, maybe...

Keep in mind that this stubbornness is teamed with a supreme confidence. Every day

The digging instinct is still strong in the Bull Terrier. This bitch is clamming for her supper!

Keep your Bull Terrier active. Running and ball playing are two favorite breed pastimes. Surely your Bull Terrier can help keep you fit if you let him.

your Bull Terrier will check the rules and test his boundaries, just in case you've decided to change them or have a memory lapse. Thankfully, though, your consistent correction results in immediate acceptance and profuse tail wagging. "Just checking," he might say.

If you don't find it unusual for a dog to attempt talking, attack inanimate objects and trick you into giving up your chair, then maybe you'll appreciate a Bull Terrier. But first keep reading as we examine some more unique and unusual habits of the Bull Terrier.

A Bull Terrier will eat just about anything he can get his teeth around, and in fact might use edibility as a criterion when judging everything in the world.

At the same time, the Bull Terrier knows what he likes in his mouth, and will do cartwheels if he has to when there's a possibility of his getting a favorite treat. However, don't try to bore a Bull Terrier with the standard liver treats, as this dog appreciates exotic cuisine. For example, have you ever seen a dog go wild over a banana? Try offering one to a Bull Terrier. Chances are the Bull Terrier will be doing backward flips before you can finish peeling the banana.

Then there is a phenomenon some owners refer to as "trancing," "ghost walking" or "weed walking." This is a strange exercise whereby your Bull Terrier is outdoors and finds a bush or patch of tall grass, and decides to "take cover." The

Bull Terriers dive right into exercise and, surprisingly, they love water sports, too.

ness and behavioral patterns that can drive some dog owners crazy cannot be overemphasized. The purpose of this book is not to scare you away from adopting a Bull Terrier, but rather to make sure that you are aware of what comes with the Bull Terrier besides a cute smile and a big head. Unfortunately, too many Bull Terriers fall to euthanasia at very young ages because their owners were not aware of, or prepared for, the breed's unique personality. On the positive side, most Bull Terrier experts agree that if you can survive the first year with your Bull Terrier, you'll be hooked for life.

THE BULL TERRIER WITH OTHER PETS

Like most other dogs, a Bull Terrier can live with other animals—provided that they

dog will walk ever so slowly underneath the bush, then stop completely still. An up-close look at the dog will reveal glazed-over eyes, as if he's in a trance, as the wind gently blows the bushes and strokes his back. Then, for no apparent reason, the dog will snap out of it, jump out of cover and continue rambling about. Some owners have witnessed this not only outdoors but indoors when the Christmas tree is up. No one seems to have come up with a logical reason for this behavior.

After discovering the Bull Terrier's unique traits, perhaps you see all of these quirks as lovable and enjoyable. If so, you may be ready to be a Bull Terrier owner!

The fact that the Bull Terrier is a very special breed with inherent quirkiness, destructive-

arrive in the home together during infancy and are raised without favoritism. However, since these conditions are quite rare, and not foolproof, you should think twice, then three times, before placing a Bull Terrier in a multi-pet household. With great strength and powerful jaws, the Bull Terrier will defend himself when faced by a perceived opponent. A confrontation with another animal, over food or toys, can result in physical damage to one or both of your beloved pets—and possibly you, when you try to intervene.

For your Bull Terrier's safety and for the safety of other animals, your Bully should not be allowed to roam free or run in an open area. The Bull Terrier is inherently aggressive toward other animals and also will be off and running if something piques his interest. Off-leash exercise should only be allowed in enclosed areas, and it is recommended that off-leash exercise be done in areas not frequented by strangers or other animals. In fact, your Bull Terrier may consider small animals like cats, rabbits, birds, gerbils and the like, and even smaller dogs, as something to be

Taking time to smell the flowers, this trio of Bull Terrier puppies is excited about exploring the world.

hunted. Keep this in mind to protect the other animals and your own dog, as you do not want him to run away from you.

Bull Terriers can be food-possessive. In multi-pet households, the Bull Terrier should be fed separately from the other animals (this includes mealtimes and treats). Do not allow any of the other pets near the Bull Terrier until you've taken the food bowl away.

With proper supervision and training, it is possible for a Bull Terrier to get along well with other animals in the home. However, it will be a fairly tedious and time-consuming effort. Bull Terriers tend to get along better with dogs of the

Though considerably larger than the Chihuahua, this Bull Terrier bitch has been properly socialized to accept her tiny playmate as a friend.

In general, terriers and rodent-type pets are best kept apart from one another, but this Bull Terrier set aside the prey instinct to snap an endearing photo.

opposite sex. A male Bully with another male dog is asking for trouble; even a two-female situation only works out sometimes. In any multiple-dog situations, equal attention must be paid to all so that jealousy does not occur.

Bull Terriers are fun for children, but the dogs must be well trained and both parties must be well behaved. This tolerant Bully soul is costumed for a night on the town.

CHILDREN AND THE BULL TERRIER

Though the Bull Terrier is a lovable, playful pet, this does not make him the perfect pal for a child—at least not without proper training and supervision. You will have much more success in raising a Bull Terrier in a home that already has children. If you've had a Bull Terrier for several years before small children are introduced into the home, there could be problems. Bull Terriers do not take kindly to the teasing, poking and pulling that children often exercise with a pet animal. Unfortunately, the Bull Terrier's first reaction to such violation is to bite—a very dangerous situation for small children who do not know any better. Be sure that your child understands that he should treat your Bull Terrier with respect. Never leave a Bull Terrier and child unsupervised. With time, training and the development of mutual respect, children and Bull Terriers not only will get along well together but also will thrive. A Bull Terrier is a happy, playful dog, always ready for anything a child cares to do. Because of his great strength and endurance, the Bull Terrier has what seems to be endless patience with children once he befriends them.

However, even if your Bull Terrier gets along quite well with your children, do not assume he will be so friendly with *all* children. Again, be sure to always supervise his activities with children.

PLAYTIME WITH YOUR BULL TERRIER

Yes, Bull Terriers like to play. If you provide a ball for your dog, make certain the ball cannot be swallowed. Tennis balls can become lodged in the dog's throat. A baseball, football or basketball will provide hours of fun. A squeak toy made from rubber or plastic can be eaten in minutes by a Bull Terrier. A hard rubber toy or nylon bone is safer. Don't provide an old pair of shoes, unless you want all of your shoes to become toys for your Bull Terrier.

Because Bull Terriers have a very strong urge to chew, it is imperative to provide them with chew toys. Appropriate toys are strong, durable chews made from nylon. Rawhides should not be given to a Bull Terrier nor should any soft toys that could be easily ripped up, swallowed or lodged in the throat. It is also essential to keep your Bull Terrier out of the garbage can, where he might discover such things as meat, fish and poultry bones from your latest meal. Keep in mind, again, that one of the first points of investigation for a Bull Terrier is "how does this taste?" They will also ingest just about anything, such as socks, pieces of blanket, hats, various types of plastic, rubber, metal and stones. Any of these items may cause obstructions in the lower intestine. If you notice symptoms, such as depression, lethargy, vomiting, diarrhea and lack of interest in food, contact your vet immediately—your Bull Terrier may have a blockage!

One of the favorite activities of a Bull Terrier is racing around the house at full speed for no apparent reason other than "just because." They rarely collide with anything unintentionally. It is almost as if they have radar as they dodge this and dodge that with great agility. Things are safest when you do not interfere.

Trying to stop a Bull Terrier is like trying to catch a greased pig. With this in mind, try to play

fetch games in an open room in the home or, better yet, outdoors, where there is less possibility of broken furniture or holes in the wall.

THE GREAT OUTDOORS

Bull Terriers have a strong need for human companionship and should be kept as house dogs— never chained or tethered

Bull Terriers love to play and are great retrievers. If you use a ball, be sure it is large enough that it cannot be swallowed by your eager Bull Terrier.

outdoors. They do not tolerate temperature extremes (both heat and cold) for long periods of time and prefer comfortable conditions. If your dog plays outdoors, off leash, your yard must be fenced or enclosed securely. Even obedience-trained Bull Terriers should not be taken off your property without a leash. They should be taken on regular walks on a sturdy lead. Bull Terriers can easily slip a regular collar, which can result in disaster in an unrestricted area, as the first thing your Bull Terrier will do is start hunting—such as anything passing by—a nearby squirrel, rabbit or, worse, a car. Some breeders recommend choke collars (used properly) for regular walks while other have found success attaching the lead to a sturdy harness.

MANAGING THE BULL TERRIER'S PERSONALITY

The Bull Terrier is most certainly devoted to his owner and family, but his loyalty can be deceiving. Although extremely affectionate and capable of making you think that you are the only one who really matters, he will go off with anyone who has a treat and a friendly voice and not even bother to look back. The Bull Terrier's personality can often be compared to that of a cat. For instance, they will sit on your lap and beg to be petted and scratched one minute,

then later they want nothing to do with you and are off by themselves to do their own thing. Bull Terriers live to please themselves. They will strive to please their owners when it benefits them. They have minds of their own and feel that it is their place to run the household. Do not underestimate the intelligence of the Bull Terrier—he knows how to get what he wants and will go to great lengths to do so.

Bull Terriers can be very spiteful and, when prevented from doing something that they wish to do, will immediately run off to find one of your most valuable possessions and do their misdeeds. They do not miss a thing and are always in the middle of what is going on. Do not trust a sleeping Bull Terrier; he is always listening, and every so often a tiny little eye slits open—just to see what's going on.

Spoiled Bull Terriers being chauffeured by their doting driver (and owner). While these two white Bullies take a handsome photograph, this is not a safe method of travel!

Being left alone for long periods of time is totally unacceptable and your Bull Terrier will let you know it. Don't be surprised when your Bull Terrier decides to chew the cushions of the chair into tiny little pieces and spit them out all over the floor. Give him about an hour and he may destroy the entire contents of your house. This is your punishment for leaving him alone.

Be forewarned: physical correction accomplishes nothing, as the Bull Terrier knows no pain. However, you may find success using a stern, scornful voice when your Bull Terrier has been bad. Watch his ears go back and his tail wag frantically as he crouches down in a submissive position, body wiggling, begging to be forgiven. It is difficult to remain angry with a Bull Terrier for very long. He will not let you! Your Bull Terrier will pester you and follow you around with those pathetic little eyes until you finally put a smile on your face and give him a loving pat. But be prepared: ten minutes later he will be right back doing whatever it was that got him in trouble in the first place.

Your Bull Terrier is often stubborn but seldom stupid and never dull. Livening things up and making everyone laugh are his specialties. Somehow, he will seem to understand what you are feeling and will do his best to cheer you up and brighten your day when you are blue.

In general, a Bull Terrier can make a good guard or watchdog because he is powerful, loyal and and determined. When a Bully barks, take notice! However, these same traits can make him jealous and overly possessive, undesirable traits that must never be encouraged. Although some Bull Terriers are so sweet that there is a better chance that an intruder will be licked to death than attacked, this scenario is not so with every dog. If a Bull Terrier senses that his master or home is being attacked, he will instantly transform into a valiant gladiator, well befitting his heritage. Due to his smaller size, he is not comparable to the larger protection dogs (such as the German Shepherd Dog or the Rottweiler), but he has the determination to

Bull Terriers live to have their own way! Stealing food and other mischievous activities can be a way of life for the Bull Terrier.

match any of these dogs and most of his bull-and-terrier cousins. Like the American Pit Bull Terrier, whose fortitude, strength and gameness are second to none, it takes great measure to stop a Bull Terrier who is fighting for his master's life or property. As duty calls, your Bull Terrier makes a grand watchdog, blessed with a booming voice that translates as fiery and serious. These traits make the Bull Terrier an ideal companion dog, since there are few canine clowns that can drop the big red nose and fright wig instantly and turn into "superdog" to protect the family he loves.

ENERGY AND ACTIVITY

The Bull Terrier is full of energy and seems to have unrelenting endurance. At the same time, the Bull Terrier is adaptable and will adjust his routine to the amount of space he is given. If you live in an apartment, he'll likely transform the living space into a Grand Prix rally track. Be aware of this if you have fragile, expensive antiques or china. If

Even a Bull Terrier knows when to take a rest. This exhausted young dog is napping after an afternoon of digging and romping on the shore.

you have a relatively small living environment, you are advised to take your Bull Terrier out to an open park or field (enclosed, of course) once or twice a week (or more often if possible) to allow this energy to run its course in less delicate surroundings.

At the same time, if you live in the country, you need to be careful in allowing your Bull Terrier to exercise freely on your farm or in your field. The Bull Terrier is naturally curious and something of a hunter. These traits may well result in mischief with a neighbor's cat or dog, or your Bull Terrier may reward you with a rabbit or squirrel for dinner. He may even run off your property. For his safety, be sure to supervise your Bull Terrier's outdoor exercise and set proper boundaries.

BULL TERRIER

A breed standard is a written description or blueprint of what the ideal specimen of a particular breed should look like. The standard allows a breeder or judge to assess a dog against what is considered to be the perfect example for that breed. Without a standard, there would be no regard to quality or breed function, and the end result would be an ever-increasing divergence from the ideal Bull Terrier.

The breed standard is the best means to measure which Bull Terriers are considered to be top-quality and which ones are considered below average. A conformation judge at a dog show is expected to evaluate each of his entries against the breed standard. It's not as easy as it sounds, and in many cases it's rather difficult to measure different degrees of faults in two dogs and decide which fault is worse than the other.

There are three main breed standards recognized and used by a majority of countries. They are The Kennel Club standard of England, the breed's native land;

the Fédération Cynologique Internationale standard, used on the Continent and elsewhere; and the American Kennel Club breed standard, used in the US and presented here. Other countries have their own breed standards, but in most cases they are minor variations of one of these three.

AMERICAN KENNEL CLUB BREED STANDARD FOR THE BULL TERRIER

WHITE
The Bull Terrier must be strongly built, muscular, symmetrical and active, with a keen determined and intelligent expression, full of

This well-bred Bull Terrier epitomizes balance, strength and musculature.

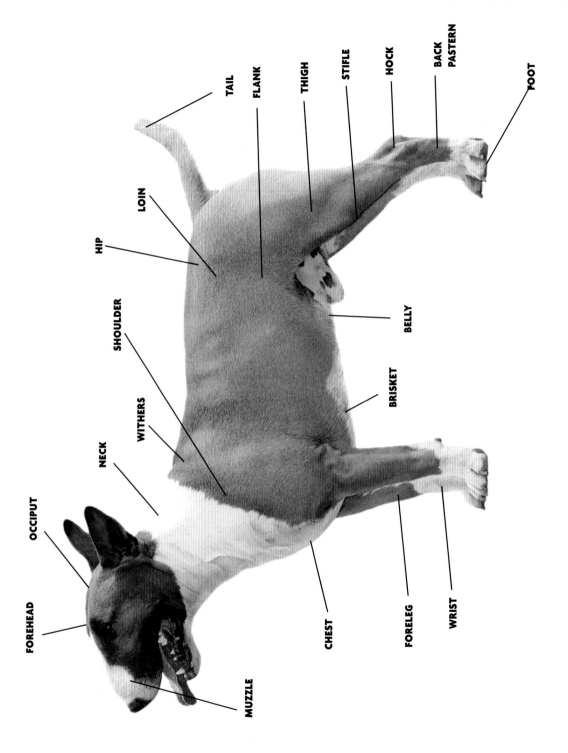

fire but of sweet disposition and amenable to discipline.

Head: Should be long, strong and deep right to the end of the muzzle, but not coarse. Full face it should be oval in outline and be filled completely up giving the impression of fullness with a surface devoid of hollows or indentations, i.e., egg shaped. In profile it should curve gently downwards from the top of the skull to the tip of the nose. The forehead should be flat across from ear to ear. The distance from the tip of the nose to the eyes should be perceptibly greater than that from the eyes to the top of the skull. The underjaw should be deep and well defined.

Lips: Should be clean and tight.

Teeth: Should meet in either a level or in a scissors bite. In the scissors bite the upper teeth should fit in front of and closely against the lower teeth, and they should be sound, strong and perfectly regular.

Ears: Should be small, thin and placed close together. They should be capable of being held stiffly erect, when they should point upwards.

Eyes: Should be well sunken and as dark as possible, with a piercing glint and they should be

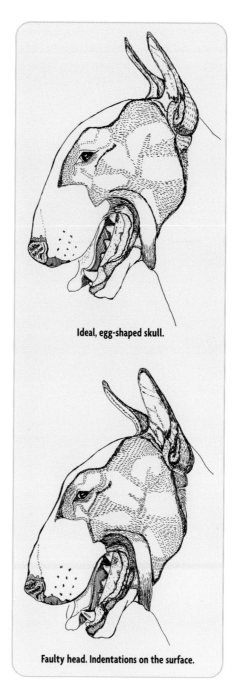

Ideal, egg-shaped skull.

Faulty head. Indentations on the surface.

Profile head study of a handsome White Bull Terrier male.

Profile head study of a lovely White Bull Terrier bitch.

Colored Bull Terrier bitch, exhibiting a nice egg-shaped head.

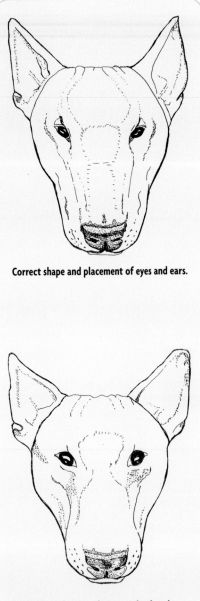

Correct shape and placement of eyes and ears.

Faults: Round eyes and incorrectly placed ears.

small, triangular and obliquely placed; set near together and high up on the dog's head. Blue eyes are a disqualification.

The Bull Terrier's front assembly should appear muscular with straight legs.

Nose: Should be black, with well-developed nostrils bent downward at the tip.

Neck: Should be very muscular, long, arched and clean, tapering from the shoulders to the head and it should be free from loose skin.

Chest: Should be broad when viewed from in front, and there should be great depth from withers to brisket, so that the latter is nearer the ground than the belly.

Body: Should be well rounded with marked spring of rib, the back should be short and strong. The back ribs deep. Slightly arched over the loin. The shoulders should be strong and muscular but without heaviness. The shoulder blades should be wide and flat and there should be a very pronounced backward slope from the bottom edge of the blade to the top edge. Behind the shoulders there should be no slackness or dip at the withers. The underline from the brisket to the belly should form a graceful upward curve.

Legs: Should be big boned but not to the point of coarseness; the

Note the clear white ground color with no tick marks on this fine Colored Bull Terrier.

upright. The hind legs should be parallel viewed from behind. The thighs very muscular with hocks well let down. Hind pasterns short and upright. The stifle joint should be well bent with a well-developed second thigh.

Feet: Round and compact with well-arched toes like a cat.

Tail: Should be short, set on low, fine, and ideally should be carried horizontally. It should be thick where it joins the body, and should taper to a fine point.

Coat: Should be short, flat, harsh to the touch and with a fine gloss. The dog's skin should fit tightly.

forelegs should be of moderate length, perfectly straight, and the dog must stand firmly upon them. The elbows must turn neither in nor out, and the pasterns should be strong and

Below: Incorrect topline.

Above: Correct back, short, arching slightly over the loin.

Color: Is white though markings on the head are permissible. Any markings elsewhere on the coat are to be severely faulted. Skin pigmentation is not to be penalized.

Movement: The dog shall move smoothly, covering the ground with free, easy strides, fore and hind legs should move parallel each to each when viewed from in front or behind. The forelegs reaching out well and the hind legs moving smoothly at the hip and flexing well at the stifle and hock. The dog should move compactly and in one piece but with a typical jaunty air that suggests agility and power.

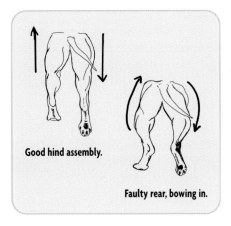

Good hind assembly.

Faulty rear, bowing in.

Faults: Any departure from the foregoing points shall be considered a fault and the seriousness of the fault shall be in exact proportion to its degree, i.e., a very crooked front is a very bad fault; a rather crooked front is a rather bad fault; and a slightly crooked front is a slight fault.
Disqualification: Blue eyes.

Colored

The Standard for the Colored Variety is the same as for the White except for the sub head "Color" which reads: Color. Any color other than white, or any color with white markings. Other things being equal, the preferred color is brindle. A dog which is predominantly white shall be disqualified.
Disqualifications: Blue eyes. Any dog which is predominantly white.

Approved July 9, 1974

MEETING THE IDEAL

The American Kennel Club defines a standard as: "A description of the ideal dog of each recognized breed, to serve as an ideal against which dogs are judged at shows." This "blueprint" is drawn up by the breed's recognized parent club, approved by a majority of its membership, and then submitted to the AKC for approval.

The AKC states that "An understanding of any breed must begin with its standard. This applies to all dogs, not just those intended for showing." The picture that the standard draws of the dog's type, gait, temperament and structure is the guiding image used by breeders as they plan their programs.

BULL TERRIER

WHERE TO BEGIN?

If you are convinced that the Bull Terrier is the ideal dog for you, it's time to learn about where to find a puppy and what to look for. Locating a litter of Bull Terriers should not present too much difficulty for the new owner. You should contact the Bull Terrier Club of America to inquire about breeders in your area who enjoy a good reputation in the breed. The Club can refer you to the type of breeder you are looking for—an established breeder with outstanding dog ethics and a

FINDING A QUALIFIED BREEDER

Before you begin your puppy search, ask for references from your veterinarian and perhaps other breeders to refer you to someone they believe is reputable. Responsible breeders usually raise only one or two breeds of dog. Avoid any breeder who has several different breeds or has several litters at the same time. Dedicated breeders are usually involved with a breed or other dog club. Many participate in some sport or activity related to their breed. Just as you want to be assured of the breeder's qualifications, the breeder wants to be assured that you will make a worthy owner. Expect the breeder to interview you, asking questions about your goals for the pup, your experience with dogs and what kind of home you will provide.

strong commitment to the breed. New owners should have as many questions as they have doubts. An established breeder is indeed the one to answer your four million questions and make you comfortable with your choice of the Bull Terrier. An established breeder will sell you a puppy at a fair price if, and only if, the breeder determines that you are a suitably worthy owner of his dogs. An

established breeder can be relied upon for advice, at any reasonable time of day or night. A reputable breeder will accept a puppy back, sometimes without penalty, should you decide that this is not the right dog for you.

When choosing a breeder, reputation is much more important than convenience of location. Do not be overly impressed by breeders who run brag advertisements in the canine publications about their stupendous champions. The quality breeders are quiet and unassuming. You hear about them at dog shows and events, by word of mouth. You may be well advised to avoid the novice who lives only a couple miles away. The local novice breeder, trying so hard to get rid of that first litter of puppies, is more than accommodating and anxious to sell you one. That breeder will charge you as much as any established breeder. The novice breeder isn't going to interrogate you and your family about your intentions with the puppy, the environment and training you can provide, etc. That breeder will be nowhere to be found when your poorly bred, badly adjusted four-pawed monster starts to growl, pick fights with the family cat and generally wreak havoc in the home.

With the Bull Terrier, socialization is a breeder concern of immense importance. Since the

Your search for a good Bull Terrier puppy should start at a kennel that is clean, well run and spacious. If the breeder does not have puppies available, you can still meet adults of the breeder's line to see how his dogs mature.

Bull Terrier's temperament can vary from line to line, socialization is the best way to encourage a proper, stable personality.

Choosing a breeder is an important first step in dog ownership. Fortunately, the majority of Bull Terrier breeders are devoted to the breed and its well-being. New owners should have little problem finding a reputable breeder who doesn't live on the other side of the country. Again, the BTCA and its affiliated clubs will help you locate breeders of quality Bull Terriers. Ethical breeders will ensure that their puppies are BAER-tested for deafness. White and Colored pups should be checked as Colored pups can be unilaterally deaf just as Whites can, though Whites can be bilaterally affected. Even normal parents can produce bilaterally deaf pups.

Once you have contacted and met a breeder or two and made your choice about which breeder is best suited to your needs, it's time to visit the litter. Keep in mind that many top breeders have waiting lists. Sometimes new owners have to wait as long as two years for a puppy. If you are really committed to the breeder whom you've selected, then you will wait (and hope for an early arrival!). If not, you may have to go with your second- or third-choice breeder. Don't be

too anxious, however. If the breeder doesn't have a waiting list, or any customers, there is probably a good reason.

Since you are likely to be choosing a Bull Terrier as a pet dog and not a show dog, you simply should select a pup that is friendly and attractive. Bull Terriers generally have medium-sized litters, averaging five puppies, so selection is somewhat limited once you have located a desirable litter. While the basic structure of the breed has little variation, the temperament may present trouble in certain strains. Beware of the shy or overly aggressive puppy; be especially conscious of the nervous Bull Terrier pup. Don't let sentiment or emotion trap you into buying the runt of the litter.

Breeders commonly allow visitors to see the litter by around the fifth or sixth week, and puppies leave for their new

Selecting the Bull Terrier puppy that you like best is never easy! Spending time with the litter and getting to know each pup is the only way to find out which pup is the best match for you.

homes between the eighth and tenth week. Breeders who permit their puppies to leave early are more interested in a profit than in their puppies' well-being. Puppies need to learn the rules of the trade from their dams, and most dams continue teaching the pups manners and dos and don'ts until at least the eighth week. Breeders spend significant amounts of time with the Bull Terrier toddlers so that they are able to interact with the "other species," i.e., humans. Given the long history that dogs and humans have, bonding between the two species is natural but must be nurtured. A well-bred, well-socialized Bull Terrier pup wants nothing more than to be near you and discover what fun you have to offer.

MEET THE PARENTS

Because puppies are a combination of genes inherited from both of their parents, they will reflect the qualities and temperament of their sire and dam. When visiting a litter of pups, spend time with the dam and observe her behavior with her puppies, the breeder and with strangers. The sire is often not on the premises, but the dam should be with her pups until they are at least eight weeks old. If either parent is surly, quarrelsome or fearful, it's likely that some of the pups will inherit those tendencies.

A COMMITTED NEW OWNER

By now you should understand what makes the Bull Terrier a most unique and special dog, one that may fit nicely into your family and lifestyle. If you have researched breeders, you should be able to recognize a knowledge-able and responsible Bull Terrier breeder who cares not only about his pups but also about what kind of owner you will be. If you have completed the final step in your new journey, you have found a litter, or possibly two, of quality Bull Terrier pups.

A visit with the puppies and their breeder should be an education in itself. Breed research, breeder selection and puppy visitation are very important aspects of finding the

PEDIGREE VS. REGISTRATION CERTIFICATE

Too often new owners are confused between these two important documents. Your puppy's pedigree, essentially a family tree, is a written record of a dog's genealogy of three generations or more. The pedigree will show you the names as well as performance titles of all dogs in your pup's background. Your breeder must provide you with a registration application, with his part properly filled out. You must complete the application and send it to the AKC with the proper fee. Every puppy must come from a litter that has been AKC-registered by the breeder, born in the US and from a sire and dam that are also registered with the AKC.

The seller must provide you with complete records to identify the puppy. The AKC requires that the seller provide the buyer with the following: breed; sex, color and markings; date of birth; litter number (when available); names and registration numbers of the parents; breeder's name; and date sold or delivered.

puppy of your dreams. Beyond that, these things also lay the foundation for a successful future with your pup. Puppy personalities within each litter vary, from the shy and easygoing puppy to the one who is dominant and assertive, with most pups falling somewhere in between. By spending time with the puppies you will be able to recognize certain behaviors and what these behaviors indicate about each pup's temperament.

Which type of pup will complement your family dynamics is best determined by observing the puppies in action within their "pack." Your breeder's expertise and recommendations are also valuable. Although you may fall in love with a bold and brassy male, the breeder may suggest that another pup would be best for you. The breeder's experience in rearing Bull Terrier pups and matching their temperaments with appropriate humans offers the best assurance that your pup will meet your needs and expectations. The type of puppy that you select is just as important as your decision that the Bull Terrier is the breed for you.

The decision to live with a Bull Terrier is a serious commitment and not one to be taken lightly. This puppy is a living sentient being that will be

How sweet! A trio of White Bull Terrier pups in a charming pose.

GETTING ACQUAINTED

When visiting a litter, ask the breeder for suggestions on how best to interact with the puppies. If possible, get right into the middle of the pack and sit down with them. Observe which pups climb into your lap and which ones shy away. Toss a toy for them to chase and bring back to you. It's easy to fall in love with the puppy who picks you, but keep your future objectives in mind before you make your final decision.

SELECTING FROM THE LITTER

Before you visit a litter of puppies, promise yourself that you won't fall for the first pretty face you see! Decide on your goals for your puppy—show prospect, obedience competitor, family companion—and then look for a puppy who displays the appropriate qualities. In most litters, there is an Alpha pup (the bossy puppy), and occasionally a shy fellow who is less confident, with the rest of the litter falling somewhere in the middle. "Middle-of-the-roaders" are safe bets for most families and novice competitors.

dependent on you for basic survival for his entire life. Beyond the basics of survival—food, water, shelter and protection—he needs much, much more. The

Just a day or so old, these Bull Terrier pups haven't even opened their eyes yet.

new pup needs love, nurturing and a proper canine education to mold him into a responsible, well-behaved canine citizen. Your Bull Terrier's health and good manners will need consistent monitoring and regular "tune-ups," so your job as a responsible dog owner will be ongoing throughout every stage of his life. If you are not prepared to accept these responsibilities and commit to them for the next decade, likely longer, then you are not prepared to own a dog of any breed.

Although the responsibilities of owning a Bull Terrier may at times tax your patience, the joy of living with this very special breed far outweighs the workload, and a well-mannered adult dog is worth your time and effort. Before your very eyes, your new charge will grow up to be your most loyal friend, devoted to you unconditionally.

YOUR BULL TERRIER SHOPPING LIST

Just as expectant parents prepare a nursery for their baby, so should you ready your home for the arrival of your Bull Terrier pup. If you have the necessary puppy supplies purchased and in place before he comes home, it will ease the puppy's transition from the warmth and familiarity of his mom and littermates to the brand-new environment of his new home and human family. You will

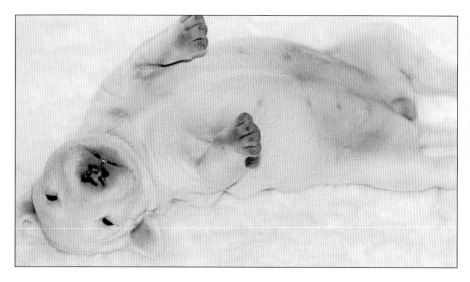

This baby Bull Terrier, helpless though she may be, would render any potential owner helplessly in love. What could be more irresistible than this darling pup?

be too busy to stock up and prepare your house after your pup comes home, that's for sure! Imagine how a pup must feel upon being transported to a strange new place. It's up to you to comfort him and to let your little pup know that he is going to be happy with you.

FOOD AND WATER BOWLS

Your puppy will need separate bowls for his food and water. Stainless steel pans are generally preferred over plastic bowls since they sterilize better and pups are less inclined to chew on the metal. Bull Terriers will certainly destroy flimsy bowls! Heavy-duty ceramic bowls are popular, but consider how often you will have to pick up those heavy bowls. Buy adult-sized pans, as your puppy will quickly grow into them.

THE DOG CRATE

If you think that crates are tools of punishment and confinement for when a dog has misbehaved, think again. Most breeders and almost all trainers recommend a crate as the preferred house-training aid as well as for all-around puppy training and safety. Because dogs are natural den creatures that prefer cave-like environments, the benefits of crate

COST OF OWNERSHIP

The purchase price of your puppy is merely the first expense in the typical dog budget. Quality dog food, veterinary care (sickness and health maintenance), dog supplies and grooming costs will add up to big bucks every year. Can you adequately afford to support a canine addition to the family?

use are many. The crate provides the puppy with his very own "safe house," a cozy place to sleep, take a break or seek comfort with a favorite toy; a travel aid to house your dog when on the road, at motels or at the vet's office; a training aid to help teach your puppy proper toileting habits; a place of solitude when non-dog people happen to drop by and don't want a lively puppy—or

Among the items you'll need for your new Bull Terrier puppy are an array of safe toys and a cozy bed or blanket where he can cuddle up.

CONFINEMENT

It is wise to keep your puppy confined to a small "puppy-proofed" area of the house for his first few weeks at home. Gate or block off a space near the door he will use for outdoor potty trips. Expandable baby gates are useful to create puppy's designated area. If he is allowed to roam through the entire house or even only several rooms, it will be more difficult to house-train him.

even a well-behaved adult dog— saying hello or begging for attention.

Crates come in several types, although the wire crate and the fiberglass airline-type crate are the most common. The wire crate is recommended for the Bull Terrier, as some may chew the fiberglass type. The wire crates also offer better visibility for the pup as well as better ventilation. Many of the wire crates easily fold down

Three crate types: mesh (left), wire (right) and fiberglass (top).

BEDDING AND CRATE PADS

Your puppy will enjoy some type of soft bedding in his "room" (the crate), something he can snuggle into to feel cozy and secure. Ample soft bedding prevents the Bully from developing pressure sores. Old towels or blankets are good choices for a young pup, since he may (and probably will) have a toileting accident or two in the crate or decide to chew on the bedding material. Once he is fully trained and out of the early chewing stage, you can replace the puppy bedding with a permanent crate pad if you prefer. Crate pads and other dog beds run the gamut from inexpensive to high-end doggie-

for easy transport. Further, the fiberglass crates do not collapse and are less ventilated than a wire crate, which can be problematic in hot weather. Some of the newer crates are made of heavy plastic mesh; they are very lightweight and fold up into slim-line suitcases. However, a Bull Terrier with a penchant for chewing could certainly chew through the mesh quickly.

Don't bother with a puppy-sized crate. Although your Bull Terrier will be a wee fellow when you bring him home, he will grow up in the blink of an eye and your puppy crate will be useless. Purchase a crate that will accommodate an adult Bull Terrier. A crate of about 36 inches long, 21–24 inches wide and 24–28 inches high will suit a fully grown Bull Terrier.

CRATE EXPECTATIONS

To make the crate more inviting to your puppy, you can offer his first meal or two inside the crate, always keeping the crate door open so that he does not feel confined. Keep a favorite toy or two in the crate for him to play with while inside. You can also cover the crate at night with a lightweight sheet to make it more den-like and remove the stimuli of household activity. Never put him into his crate as punishment or as you are scolding him, since he will then associate his crate with negative situations and avoid going there.

Invest in a sturdy crate, as you'll be using it for a long time.

styles, but don't splurge on the good stuff until you are sure that your puppy is reliable and won't tear it up or make a mess on it.

PUPPY TOYS

Just as infants and older children require objects to stimulate their minds and bodies, puppies need toys to entertain their curious brains, wiggly paws and achy teeth. A fun array of safe doggie toys will help satisfy your puppy's chewing instincts and distract him from gnawing on the leg of your antique chair or your new leather sofa. Most puppy toys are cute and look as if they would be a lot of fun, but not all are necessarily safe or good for your puppy, so use caution when you go puppy-toy shopping.

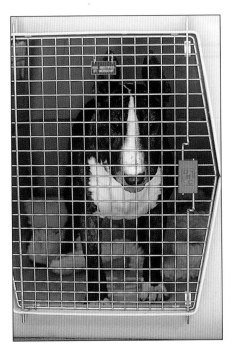

Bull Terrier puppies and adults are aggressive chewers and only the hardest, strongest toys should be offered to them. The best "chewcifiers" are nylon and hard rubber bones; many are safe to gnaw on and come in sizes appropriate for all age groups and breeds. Avoid offering natural bones, which can splinter or develop dangerous sharp edges; a dog can easily swallow or choke on those bone splinters. Veterinarians often tell of surgical nightmares involving bits of splintered bone, because in addition to the danger of choking, the sharp pieces can damage the intestinal tract.

MAKE A COMMITMENT

Dogs are most assuredly man's best friend, but they are also a lot of work. When you add a puppy to your family, you also are adding to your daily responsibilities for years to come. Dogs need more than just food, water and a place to sleep. They also require training (which can be ongoing throughout the lifetime of the dog), activity to keep them physically and mentally fit and hands-on attention every day, plus grooming and health care. Your life as you now know it may well disappear! Are you prepared for such drastic changes?

Similarly, rawhide chews, while a favorite of most dogs and puppies, are equally dangerous for Bull Terriers. Pieces of rawhide are easily swallowed after they get soft and gummy from chewing, and dogs have been known to choke on large pieces of ingested rawhide or suffer from blockages.

Soft woolly toys are not advised for Bull Terriers either. They come in a wide variety of cute shapes and sizes; some look like little stuffed animals.

However, these fuzzy toys often have button eyes or noses that your Bully can chew off and swallow. Furthermore, squeaky toys can easily be ripped open so that the dog can remove the squeake. Braided rope toys are fun to chew and toss around, but should only be offered under supervision as they shred easily and the strings are easy to swallow. The strings are not digestible and, if the puppy doesn't pass them in his stool, he could end up at the vet's office.

Wire crates provide excellent ventilation and visibility for the dog. They can be taken apart or folded for easy transport and quickly reassembled.

TOYS 'R SAFE

The vast array of tantalizing puppy toys is staggering. Stroll through any pet shop or pet-supply outlet and you will see that the choices can be overwhelming. However, not all dog toys are safe or sensible. Avoid toys that have buttons, tabs or other enhancements that can be chewed off and swallowed. Also make sure your puppy does not disembowel a squeaky toy and remove (and swallow) the squeaker. Toys that rattle or make noise can excite a puppy, but they present the same danger as the squeaky kind and so require supervision. Hard rubber toys that bounce can also entertain a pup, but make sure that the toy is too big for your pup to swallow.

If you believe that your pup has ingested a piece of a toy or another forbidden object, check his stools for the next couple of days to see if he passes the item when he defecates. At the same time, also watch for signs of intestinal distress. A call to your vet might be in order to get his advice and be on the safe side.

An all-time favorite toy for puppies (young and old!) is the empty gallon milk jug. Hard plastic juice containers—46 ounces or more—are also excellent. Such containers make lots of noise when they are batted about, and puppies go crazy with delight as they play with them. However, these won't last longer than a few minutes with a Bully, so be sure to remove them as soon as they get chewed up.

A word of caution about homemade toys: be careful with your choices of non-traditional play objects. Never use old shoes or socks, since a puppy cannot distinguish between the old ones on which he's allowed to chew and the new ones in your closet that are strictly off limits. That principle applies to anything that resembles something that you don't want your puppy to chew.

COLLARS

A lightweight nylon collar is the best choice for a very young pup. Quick-clip collars are easy to put on and remove, and they can be adjusted as the puppy grows. Introduce him to his collar as soon as he comes home to get him accustomed to wearing it. He'll get used to it quickly and won't mind a bit. Make sure that it is snug enough that it won't slip off, yet loose enough to be comfortable for the pup. You should be able to slip two fingers between the collar and his neck. Check the collar often, as puppies grow in spurts, and his collar can

become too tight almost overnight. Choke collars are for training purposes and should never be left on a dog. Further, a choke collar should never be used on a puppy and should only be used by an owner who knows exactly how to use it correctly.

LEASHES

A 6-foot nylon lead is an excellent choice for a young puppy. It is lightweight and not as tempting to chew as a leather lead. You can

COLLARING OUR CANINES

The standard flat collar with a buckle or a snap, in leather, nylon or cotton, is widely regarded as the everyday all-purpose collar. If the collar fits correctly, you should be able to fit two fingers between the collar and the dog's neck.

Leather Buckle Collars

The martingale, Greyhound or limited-slip collar is preferred by many dog owners and trainers. It is fixed with an extra loop that tightens when pressure is applied to the leash. The martingale collar gets tighter but does not "choke" the dog. The limited-slip collar should only be used for walking and training, not for free play or interaction with another dog. These types of collar should never be left on the dog, as the extra loop can lead to accidents.

Choke collars, usually made of stainless steel, are made for training purposes but are not recommended for small dogs or heavily coated breeds. The chains can injure small dogs or damage long/abundant coats. Thin nylon choke leads are commonly used on show dogs while in the ring, though they are not practical for everyday use.

The harness, with two or three straps that attach over the dog's shoulders and around his torso, is a humane and safe alternative to the conventional collar. By and large, a well-made harness is virtually escape-proof. Harnesses are available in nylon and mesh and can be outfitted on most dogs, with chest girths ranging from 10 to 30 inches.

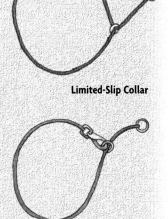

Limited-Slip Collar

Snap Bolt Choke Collar

Harness

Nylon Collar

Quick-Click Closure

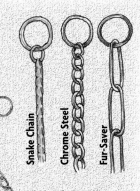

Snake Chain

Chrome Steel

Fur-Saver

Choke Chain Collars

A head collar, composed of a nylon strap that goes around the dog's muzzle and a second strap that wraps around his neck, offers the owner better control over his dog. This device is recommended for problem-solving with dogs (including jumping up, pulling and aggressive behaviors), but must be used with care.

A training halter, including a flat collar and two straps, made of nylon and webbing, is designed for walking. There are several on the market; some are more difficult to put on the dog than others. The halter harness, with two small slip rings at each end, is recommended for ease of use.

Games of tugging are not recommended for the Bull Terrier. They promote the breed's stubborn "bull headed" nature.

switch to a 6-foot leather lead after your pup has grown and is used to walking politely on a lead. For initial puppy walks and house-training purposes, you should invest in a shorter lead so that you have more control over the puppy. At first, you don't want him wandering too far away

from you, and when taking him out for toileting you will want to keep him in the specific area chosen for his potty spot.

HOME SAFETY FOR YOUR PUPPY
The importance of puppy-proofing cannot be overstated. In addition to making your house comfortable for your Bull Terrier's arrival, you also must make sure that your house is safe for your puppy before you bring him home. There are countless hazards in the owner's personal living environment that a curious Bull Terrier pup can sniff, chew, swallow or destroy. Many are obvious; others are not. Do a thorough advance house check to remove or rearrange those things that could hurt your puppy, keeping any potentially dangerous items out of areas to which he will have access. Remember that the Bull Terrier is quite a talented investigator and he explores with his mouth!

A harness is an excellent option for walking a Bull Terrier. Here's the very macho Ywis Brindle Spot, owned by J. Bergman, showing off his sturdy leather accessories.

LEASH LIFE

Dogs love leashes! Believe it or not, most dogs dance for joy every time their owners pick up their leashes. The leash means that the dog is going for a walk—and there are few things more exciting than that! Here are some of the kinds of leashes that are commercially available.

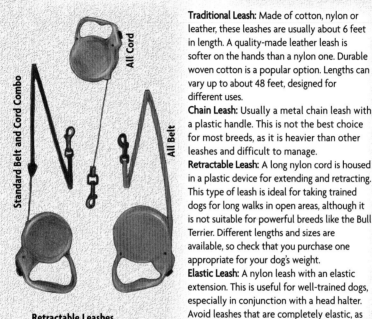

Nylon Leash

Leather Leash

Traditional Leash: Made of cotton, nylon or leather, these leashes are usually about 6 feet in length. A quality-made leather leash is softer on the hands than a nylon one. Durable woven cotton is a popular option. Lengths can vary up to about 48 feet, designed for different uses.

Chain Leash: Usually a metal chain leash with a plastic handle. This is not the best choice for most breeds, as it is heavier than other leashes and difficult to manage.

Retractable Leash: A long nylon cord is housed in a plastic device for extending and retracting. This type of leash is ideal for taking trained dogs for long walks in open areas, although it is not suitable for powerful breeds like the Bull Terrier. Different lengths and sizes are available, so check that you purchase one appropriate for your dog's weight.

Elastic Leash: A nylon leash with an elastic extension. This is useful for well-trained dogs, especially in conjunction with a head halter. Avoid leashes that are completely elastic, as

they afford minimal control to the handler.

Adjustable Leash: This has two snaps, one on each end, and several metal rings. It is handy if you need to tether your dog temporarily, but is never to be used with a choke collar.

Tab Leash: A short leash (4 to 6 inches long) that attaches to your dog's collar. This device serves like a handle, in case you have to grab your dog while he's exercising off lead. It's ideal for "half-trained" dogs or dogs that listen only half of the time.

Slip Leash: Essentially a leash with a collar built in, similar to what a dog-show handler uses to show a dog. This British-style collar has a ring on the end so that you can form a slip collar. Useful if you have to catch your own runaway dog or a stray.

Standard Belt and Cord Combo

All Cord

All Belt

Retractable Leashes

All Cord

Chrome Chain

Chain with Spring

Adjustable Lead with Swivel

Loop with Sliding Bead

Martingale / Humane Choke

Show Lead with Sliding Clasp

Slip Noose

A Variety of Collar-and-Leash-in-One Products

Electrical cords are especially dangerous, since puppies view them as irresistible chew toys. Unplug and remove all exposed cords or fasten them beneath a baseboard where the puppy cannot reach them. Veterinarians and firefighters can tell you horror stories about electrical burns and house fires that resulted from puppy-chewed electrical cords. Consider this a most serious precaution for your puppy and the rest of your family.

Scout your home for tiny objects that might be seen at a pup's eye level. Keep medication bottles and cleaning supplies well out of reach, and do the same with waste baskets and other trash containers. It goes without saying that you should not use rodent poison or other toxic chemicals in any puppy area and that you must keep such containers safely locked up. You will be amazed at how many places a curious puppy can discover!

Once your house has cleared inspection, check your yard. A sturdy fence will give your dog a safe place to play and potty. The fence must be well-embedded into the ground so that a tenacious

"You're white, you're on a leash, but you're not a Bull Terrier!" This Bully looks happy to meet a barnyard friend. All introductions to other animals should be done on-lead.

A Dog-Safe Home

The dog-safety police are taking you and your new puppy on a house tour. Let's go room by room and see how safe your own home is for your new pup. The following items are doggie dangers, so either they must be removed or the dog should be monitored or not allowed access to these areas.

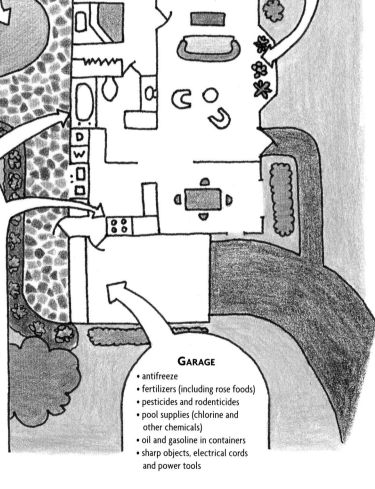

Living Room
- house plants (some varieties are poisonous)
- fireplace or wood-burning stove
- paint on the walls (lead-based paint is toxic)
- lead drapery weights (toxic lead)
- lamps and electrical cords
- carpet cleaners or deodorizers

Outdoors
- swimming pool
- pesticides
- toxic plants
- lawn fertilizers

Bathroom
- blue water in the toilet bowl
- medicine cabinet (filled with potentially deadly bottles)
- soap bars, bleach, drain cleaners, etc.
- tampons

Kitchen
- household cleaners in the kitchen cabinets
- glass jars and canisters
- sharp objects (like kitchen knives, scissors and forks)
- garbage pail (with remnants of good-smelling things like onions, potato skins, apple or pear cores, peach pits, coffee beans and other harmful tidbits.)
- food left out on counters (some foods are toxic to dogs)

Garage
- antifreeze
- fertilizers (including rose foods)
- pesticides and rodenticides
- pool supplies (chlorine and other chemicals)
- oil and gasoline in containers
- sharp objects, electrical cords and power tools

TOXIC PLANTS

Plants are natural puppy magnets, but many can be harmful, even fatal, if ingested by a puppy or adult dog. Scout your yard and home interior and remove any plants, bushes or flowers that could be even mildly dangerous. It could save your puppy's life. You can obtain a complete list of toxic plants from your veterinarian, at the public library or by looking online.

digger cannot burrow under—remember that terriers are "earth dogs." Although Bull Terriers are not known to be climbers or fence jumpers, they are still athletic dogs, so a 5- to 6-foot-high fence is required to contain an agile youngster or adult. Check the fence periodically for necessary repairs. If there is a weak link or space to squeeze through, you can be sure a determined Bull Terrier will discover it.

The garage and shed can be hazardous places for a pup, as things like fertilizers, chemicals and tools are usually kept there. It's best to keep these areas off limits to the pup. Antifreeze is especially dangerous to dogs, as they find the taste appealing and it takes only a few licks from the driveway to kill a dog, puppy or adult, small breed or large.

VISITING THE VETERINARIAN

A good veterinarian is your Bull Terrier puppy's best health-insurance policy. If you do not already have a vet, ask friends and experienced dog people in your area for recommendations so that you can select a vet before you bring your Bull Terrier puppy home. Also arrange for your puppy's first veterinary examination beforehand, since many vets have two- and three-week waiting periods and your puppy should visit the vet within a day or so of coming home.

Sprouting up to steal your heart is an adorable Bully pup!

It's important to make sure your puppy's first visit to the vet is a pleasant and positive one. The vet should take great care to befriend the pup and handle him gently to make their first meeting a positive experience. The vet will give the pup a thorough physical examination and set up a schedule for vaccinations and other necessary wellness visits. Be sure to show your vet any health and inoculation records, which you should have received from your breeder. Your vet is a great source of canine health information, so be sure to ask questions and take notes. Creating a health journal for your puppy will make a handy reference for his wellness and any future health problems that may arise.

MEETING THE FAMILY

Your Bull Terrier's homecoming is an exciting time for all members of the family, and it's only natural that everyone will be eager to meet him, pet him and play with him. However, for the puppy's sake, it's best to make these initial family meetings as uneventful as possible so that the pup is not overwhelmed with too much too soon. Remember, he has just left his dam and his littermates and is away from the breeder's home for the first time. Despite his constantly wagging tail, he is still apprehensive and wondering where he is and who all these

strange humans are. It's best to let him explore on his own and meet the family members as he feels comfortable. Let him investigate all the new smells, sights and sounds at his own pace. Children should be especially careful to not get overly excited, use loud voices or hug the pup too tightly. Be calm, gentle and affectionate, and be ready to comfort him if he appears frightened or uneasy.

Be sure to show your puppy his new crate during this first day home. Toss a treat or two inside the crate; if he associates the crate with food, he will associate the crate with good things. If he is comfortable with the crate, you

PUPPY PARASITES

Parasites are nasty little critters that live in or on your dog or puppy. Most puppies are born with ascarid roundworms, which are acquired from dormant ascarids residing in the dam. Other parasites can be acquired through contact with infected fecal matter. Take a stool sample to your vet for testing. He will prescribe a safe wormer to treat any parasites found in your puppy's stool. Always have a fecal test performed at your puppy's annual veterinary exam.

can offer him his first meal inside it. Leave the door ajar so he can wander in and out as he chooses.

FIRST NIGHT IN HIS NEW HOME

So much has happened in your Bull Terrier puppy's first day away from the breeder. He's had his first car ride to his new home. He's met his new human family and perhaps the other family pets. He has explored his new house and yard, at least those places where he is to be allowed during his first weeks at home. He may have visited his new veterinarian. He has eaten his first meal or two away from his dam and litter-mates. Surely that's enough to tire

out an eight-week-old Bull Terrier pup…so you hope!

It's bedtime. During the day, the pup investigated his crate, which is his new den and sleeping space, so it is not entirely strange to him. Line the crate with a soft towel or blanket that he can snuggle into and gently place him into the crate for the night. Some breeders send home a piece of bedding from where the pup slept with his littermates, and those familiar scents are a great comfort for the puppy on his first night without his siblings.

He will probably whine or cry. The puppy is objecting to the confinement and the fact that he is alone for the first time. This can be a stressful time for you as well as for the pup. It's important that you remain strong and don't let the puppy out of his crate to comfort him. He will fall asleep eventually. If you release him, the puppy will learn that crying means "out" and will continue that habit. You are laying the

Puppies learn important life lessons by playing with their siblings. They will miss the company of their littermates when they first go to new homes.

ASK THE VET

Help your vet help you to become a well-informed dog owner. Don't be shy about becoming involved in your puppy's veterinary care by asking questions and gaining as much knowledge as you can. For starters, ask what shots your puppy is getting and what diseases they prevent, and discuss with your vet the safest way to vaccinate. Find out what is involved in your dog's annual wellness visits. If you plan to spay or neuter, discuss the best age at which to have this done. Start out on the right "paw" with your puppy's vet and develop good communication with him, as he will care for your dog's health throughout the dog's entire life.

DIGGING OUT

Digging is considered "self-rewarding" because it's fun! Of all the digging solutions offered by the experts, most are only marginally successful and none is guaranteed to work. The best cure is prevention, which means removing the dog from the offending site when he digs as well as distracting him when you catch him digging so that he turns his attentions elsewhere. That means supervising your dog's yard time.

groundwork for future habits. Some breeders find that soft music can soothe a crying pup and help him get to sleep.

SOCIALIZING YOUR PUPPY

The first 20 weeks of your Bull Terrier puppy's life are the most important of his entire lifetime. A properly socialized Bull Terrier puppy will grow up to be a confident and stable adult who will be a pleasure to live with and a welcome addition to the neighborhood.

The importance of socialization with the Bull Terrier cannot be overemphasized to encourage a stable disposition. Research on canine behavior has proven that puppies who are not exposed to new sights, sounds, people and animals during their first 20 weeks of life will grow up to be timid and fearful, even aggressive, and unable to flourish outside of their home environment.

Socializing your puppy is not difficult and, in fact, will be a fun time for you both. Lead training goes hand in hand with socialization, so your puppy will be learning how to walk on a lead at the same time that he's meeting the neighborhood. Because the Bull Terrier is such a terrific breed, people will enjoy meeting "the new kid on the block." Take him for short walks, to the park and to other dog-friendly places where he will encounter new people, especially children. Puppies automatically recognize children as "little people" and are drawn to play with them. Just make sure that you supervise these meetings and that the children do not get too rough or encourage him to play too hard. An overzealous pup can often nip too hard, frightening the child and in turn making the puppy overly excited. A bad experience in puppyhood can impact a dog for life, so a pup that has a negative experience with a child may grow up to be shy or even aggressive around children.

Take your puppy along on your daily errands. Puppies are natural "people magnets," and most people who see your pup will want to pet him. All of these encounters will help to mold him into a confident adult dog. Likewise, you will soon feel like a confident, responsible dog owner, rightly proud of your handsome Bull Terrier.

Be especially careful of your puppy's encounters and experiences during the eight-to-ten-week-old period, which is also called the "fear period." This is a serious imprinting period, and all contact during this time should be gentle and positive. A frightening or negative event could leave a permanent impression that could affect his future behavior if a similar situation arises.

Also make sure that your puppy has received his first and second rounds of vaccinations before you expose him to other dogs or bring him to places that other dogs may frequent. Although socialization with other canines is essential, you should avoid dog parks and other strange-dog areas until your vet assures you that your puppy is fully immunized and resistant to the diseases that can be passed between canines. Discuss socialization with your breeder, as some breeders recommend socializing the puppy even before he has received all of his inoculations, depending on how outgoing the puppy may be.

LEADER OF THE PUPPY'S PACK

Like other canines, your puppy needs an authority figure, someone he can look up to and regard as the leader of his "pack."

His first pack leader was his dam, who taught him to be polite and not chew too hard on her ears or nip at her muzzle. He learned those same lessons from his littermates. If he played too rough, they cried in pain and stopped the game, which sent an important message to the rowdy puppy.

As puppies play together, they are also struggling to determine who will be the boss. Being pack animals, dogs need someone to be in charge. If a litter of puppies remained together beyond puppyhood, one of the pups would emerge as the strongest one, the one who calls the shots.

Once your puppy leaves the pack, he will look intuitively for a new leader. If he does not recognize you as that leader, he will try to assume that position for himself. Of course, it is hard to imagine your adorable Bull Terrier puppy trying to be in charge when

CREATE A SCHEDULE

Puppies thrive on sameness and routine. Offer meals at the same time each day, take him out at regular times for potty trips and do the same for play periods and outdoor activity. Make note of when your puppy naps and when he is most lively and energetic, and try to plan his day around those times. Once he is house-trained and more predictable in his habits, he will be better able to tolerate changes in his schedule.

he is so small and seemingly helpless, but the Bull Terrier is a determined dog. You must remember that these are natural breed instincts. Do not cave in and allow your Bully pup to "bully" you around!

Just as socialization is so important during these first 20 weeks, so too is your puppy's early education. He was born without any bad habits. He does not know what is good or bad behavior. If he does things like nipping and digging, it's because he is having fun and doesn't know that humans consider these things as "bad." It's your job to teach him proper puppy manners, and this is the best time to accomplish that...before he has developed bad habits, since it is much more difficult to "unlearn" or correct unacceptable learned behavior than to teach good behavior from the start.

Make sure that all members of the family understand the importance of being consistent when training their new puppy. If you tell the puppy to stay off the sofa and your daughter allows him to cuddle with her on the couch to watch her favorite television show, your pup will be confused about what he is and is not allowed to do. Have a family conference before your pup comes home so that everyone understands the basic principles of puppy training and the rules you have set forth for the pup, and agrees to follow them.

The old saying that "an ounce of prevention is worth a pound of cure" is especially true when it comes to puppies. It is much easier to prevent inappropriate behavior than it is to change it. It's also easier and less stressful for the pup, since it will keep discipline to a minimum and create a more positive learning environment for him. That, in turn, will also be easier on you!

SOLVING PUPPY PROBLEMS

CHEWING AND NIPPING

Nipping at fingers and toes is normal puppy behavior. Chewing is also the way that puppies investigate their surroundings. However, you will have to teach your puppy that chewing anything other than his toys is not acceptable. That won't happen overnight and at times puppy teeth will test your patience. However, if you allow nipping and chewing to continue, just think about the damage that a mature Bull Terrier can do with a full set of powerful adult terrier teeth.

Whenever your puppy nips your hand or fingers, cry out "Ouch!" in a loud voice, which should startle your puppy and stop him from nipping, even if only for a moment. Immediately distract him by offering a small treat or an appropriate toy for him to chew instead (which means having chew toys and puppy treats handy or in your pockets at all times). Praise him when he takes the toy and tell him what a good fellow he is. Praise is just as or even more important in puppy training as discipline and correction. Bullies thrive on positive reinforcement.

Puppies also tend to nip at children more often than adults, since they perceive little ones to be more vulnerable and more similar to their littermates. Teach your children appropriate responses to nipping behavior. If they are unable to handle it themselves, you may have to intervene. Puppy nips can be quite painful and a child's frightened reaction will only encourage

Among all of their unique personality traits, Bull Terriers are lovable and affectionate pets who love to be as close to their people as possible.

a puppy to nip harder, which is a natural canine response. As with all other puppy situations, interaction between your Bull Terrier puppy and children should be supervised.

Chewing on objects, not just family members' fingers and ankles, is also normal canine behavior that can be especially tedious (for the owner, not the pup) during the teething period when the puppy's adult teeth are coming in. At this stage, chewing just plain feels good. Furniture legs and cabinet corners are common puppy favorites. Shoes and other personal items also taste pretty good to a pup.

The best solution is, once again, prevention. If you value something, keep it tucked away and out of reach. You can't hide your dining-room table in a closet, but you can try to deflect the chewing by applying a bitter product made just to deter dogs from chewing. Available in a

BE CONSISTENT

Consistency is a key element, in fact is absolutely necessary, to a puppy's learning environment. A behavior (such as chewing, jumping up or climbing onto the furniture) cannot be forbidden one day and then allowed the next. That will only confuse the pup, and he will not understand what he is supposed to do. Just one or two episodes of allowing an undesirable behavior to "slide" will imprint that behavior on a puppy's brain and make that behavior more difficult to erase or change.

spray or cream, this substance is vile-tasting, although safe for dogs, and most puppies will avoid the forbidden object after one tiny taste. You also can apply the product to your leather leash if the puppy tries to chew on his lead during leash-training sessions.

Keep a ready supply of safe chews handy to offer your Bull Terrier as a distraction when he starts to chew on something that's a "no-no." Remember, at this tender age he does not yet know what is permitted or forbidden, so you have to be "on call" every minute he's awake and on the prowl.

You may lose a treasure or two during puppy's growing-up period, and the furniture could sustain a nasty nick or two. These can be trying times, so be prepared for those inevitable accidents and comfort yourself in knowing that this too shall pass.

PUPPY WHINING

Puppies often cry and whine, just as infants and little children do. It's their way of telling us that they are lonely or in need of attention. Bull Terriers thrive on companionship of their families and will be very unhappy without it. Your puppy will miss his litter-mates and will feel insecure when he is left alone. You may

be out of the house or just in another room, but he will still feel alone. During these times, the puppy's crate should be his personal comfort station, a place all his own where he can feel safe and secure. Once he learns that being alone is okay and not something to be feared, he will settle down without crying or objecting. You might want to leave a radio on while he is crated, as the sound of human voices can be soothing and will give the impression that people are around.

Give your puppy a favorite sturdy chew toy and even a crunchy dog treat to entertain him whenever he is crated. You will both be happier: the puppy because he is safe in his den and you because he is quiet, safe and not getting into puppy escapades that can wreak havoc in your house or cause him danger.

To make sure that your puppy will always view his crate as a safe and cozy place, never, ever, use the crate as punishment. That's the best way to turn the crate into a negative place that the pup will want to avoid. Sure, you can use the crate for your own peace of mind if your puppy is getting into trouble and needs some "time out." Just don't let him know that! Never scold the pup and immediately place him into the crate. Count to ten, give him a couple of hugs and maybe a treat, then scoot him into his crate.

It's also important not to make a big fuss when he is released from the crate. That will make getting out of the crate more appealing than being in the crate, which is just the opposite of what you are trying to achieve.

"COUNTER SURFING"

What we like to call "counter surfing" is a normal activity for many dogs and usually starts to happen as soon as a puppy realizes that he is big enough to stand on his hind legs and investigate the good stuff on the kitchen counter or the coffee table. Once again, you have to be there to prevent it! As soon as you see your Bull Terrier even start to raise himself up, startle him with a sharp "No!" or "Aaahh, aaahh!" If he succeeds and manages to get one or both paws on the forbidden surface, smack those paws (firmly but gently) and tell him "Off!" As soon as he's back on all four paws, command him to sit and praise at once.

For surf prevention, make sure to keep any tempting treats or edibles out of reach, where your Bull Terrier can't see or smell them. It's the old rule of prevention yet again.

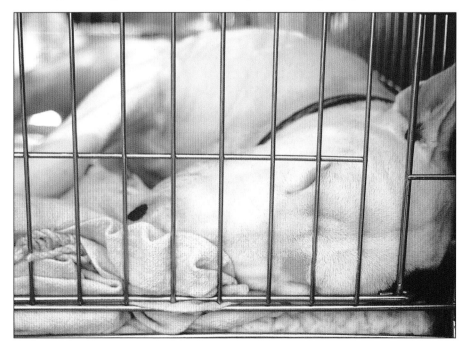

If you crate-train your Bull Terrier as a puppy, he will enjoy his crate throughout his life.

Adding a Bull Terrier to your household means adding a new family member who will need your care each and every day. When your Bull Terrier pup first comes home, you will start a routine with him so that, as he grows up, your dog will have a daily schedule just as you do. The aspects of your dog's daily care will likewise become regular parts of your day, so you'll both have a new schedule. Dogs learn by consistency and thrive on routine:

regular times for meals, exercise, grooming and potty trips are just as important for your dog as they are to you! Your dog's schedule will depend much on your family's daily routine, but remember that you now have a new member of the family who is part of your day every day.

FEEDING

Feeding your dog the best diet is based on various factors, including age, activity level, overall condition and size of breed. When you visit the breeder, he will share with you his advice about the proper diet for your dog based on his experience with the breed and the foods with which he has had success. Likewise, your vet will be a helpful source of advice throughout the dog's life and will aid you in planning a diet for optimal health.

There is a great deal of information available on dog nutrition. The simplest way to feed your dog well is to find a quality dry dog food which your dog seems to enjoy, and stick with that brand. Cheap dog food is no bargain! Without sufficient quantities of all required nutrients, your Bull Terrier may never grow to his full potential and may develop

---

NOT HUNGRY?

No dog in his right mind would turn down his dinner, would he? If you notice that your dog has lost interest in his food, there could be any number of causes. Dental problems are a common cause of appetite loss, one that is often overlooked. If your dog has a toothache, a loose tooth or sore gums from infection, chances are it doesn't feel so good to chew. Think about when you've had a toothache! If your dog does not approach the food bowl with his usual enthusiasm, look inside his mouth for signs of a problem. Whatever the cause, you'll want to consult your vet so that your chow hound can get back to his happy, hungry self as soon as possible.

various ailments associated with poor nutrition. For example, the expense involved in trying to clear up skin and coat problems related to lack of certain fats and fatty acids in the diet quickly uses up the money saved by purchasing poor-quality food.

Some Bull Terrier owners prefer to feed a natural diet that they create themselves. If this is carefully done, the results can be excellent, but the owner has to

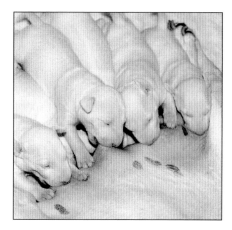

Bull Terrier puppies suckle from their mother for about the first six weeks of their lives. Weaning is usually complete by the seventh or eighth week.

have the time, education and dedication to do it properly. The owner must make sure that the diet contains complete nutrition in proper proportions!

As a rule, Bull Terriers are good eaters. In fact, some are gluttons! Try not to let your dog become too heavy. If you are unfortunate enough to have a picky eater, first make sure that there is no medical reason for his uninterest in food. For instance, tooth problems may make a dog reluctant to eat hard food. If there is no medical explanation, your Bully is probably holding out for whatever his human family is having for dinner! You simply have to be more stubborn than he is. Keep giving him his quality dog food, and hopefully he'll soon get the message.

FEEDING THE PUPPY

Of course, your pup's very first food will be his dam's milk. There

SWITCHING FOODS

There are certain times in a dog's life when it becomes necessary to switch his food; for example, from puppy to adult food and then from adult to senior-dog food. Additionally, you may decide to feed your pup a different type of food from what he received from the breeder, and there may be "emergency" situations in which you can't find your dog's normal brand and have to offer something else temporarily. Anytime a change is made, for whatever reason, the switch must be done gradually. You don't want to upset the dog's stomach or end up with a picky eater who refuses to eat something new. A tried-and-true approach is, over the course of about a week, to mix a little of the new food in with the old, increasing the proportion of new to old as the days progress. At the end of the week, you'll be feeding his regular portions of the new food, and he will barely notice the change.

they snatch bites from their mom's food bowl.

By the time the pups are ready for new homes, they are fully weaned and eating a good puppy food. As a new owner, you may be thinking, "Great! The breeder has taken care of the hard part." Not so fast.

A puppy's first year of life is the time when all or most of his growth and development takes place. This is a delicate time, and diet plays a huge role in proper skeletal and muscular formation. Improper diet and exercise habits can lead to damaging problems that will compromise the dog's health and movement for his entire life. That being said, new owners should not worry needlessly. With the myriad types of food formulated specifically for growing pups of different-sized breeds, dog-food manufacturers have taken much of the guesswork out of feeding your puppy well. Since growth-food formulas are designed to provide the nutrition that a growing puppy needs, it is

It is best to continue with the same diet used by the breeder until your Bull Terrier is ready to make the switch to adult dog food.

may be special situations in which pups fail to nurse, necessitating that the breeder hand-feed them with a formula, but, for the most part, pups spend the first weeks of life nursing from their dam. The breeder weans the pups by gradually introducing solid foods and decreasing the milk meals. Pups may even start themselves off on the weaning process, albeit inadvertently, if

Sturdy stainless steel dishes are recommended for the Bull Terrier's food and water, as he may turn a less durable bowl into a chew toy!

that dividing the day's food into two meals on a morning/evening schedule is healthier for the dog's digestion than one large meal.

Regarding the feeding schedule, feeding the pup at the same times and in the same place each day is important for both housebreaking purposes and establishing the dog's everyday routine. As for the amount to feed, growing puppies generally need proportionately more food per body weight than their adult counterparts, but a pup should never be allowed to gain excess weight. Dogs of all ages should be kept in proper body condition, but extra weight can strain a pup's developing frame, causing skeletal problems.

Watch your pup's weight as he grows and, if the recommended amounts seem to be too much or too little for your pup, consult the

Discuss the diet of your adult Bull Terrier with your vet. As an active breed, Bull Terriers likely have different nutritional requirements from dogs with lower activity levels.

unnecessary and, in fact, can prove harmful to add supplements to the diet. Research has shown that too much of certain vitamin supplements and minerals predispose a dog to skeletal problems. It's by no means a case of "if a little is good, a lot is better." At every stage of your dog's life, too much or too little in the way of nutrients can be harmful, which is why a manufactured complete food is the easiest way to know that your dog is getting what he needs.

Because of a young pup's small body and accordingly small digestive system, his daily portion will be divided up into small meals throughout the day. This can mean starting off with three or more meals a day and decreasing the number of meals as the pup matures. For the adult's feeding schedule, it is generally thought

TOXIC TREATS
Small amounts of fresh grapes and raisins can cause vomiting and diarrhea in dogs, possibly even kidney failure in the worst cases. Nuts, in general, are not recommended for dogs. Macadamia nuts, for example, can cause vomiting, diarrhea, fatigue and temporary paralysis of rear legs. Dogs usually recover from these symptoms in a few days. Almonds are also especially problematic for dogs. Onions can be deadly to dogs, causing a very serious type of anemia.

vet about appropriate dietary changes. Keep in mind that treats, although small, can quickly add up throughout the day, contributing unnecessary calories. Treats are fine when used prudently; opt for dog treats specially formulated to be healthy or for nutritious snacks like small pieces of cheese or cooked chicken.

FEEDING THE ADULT DOG

For the adult (meaning physically mature) dog, feeding properly is about maintenance, not growth. Again, correct weight is a concern. Your dog should appear fit and should have an evident "waist." His ribs should not be protruding (a sign of being underweight), but they should be covered by only a slight layer of fat. Under normal circumstances, an adult dog can be maintained fairly easily with a high-quality nutritionally complete adult-formula food.

Factor treats into your dog's overall daily caloric intake, and avoid offering table scraps. Overweight dogs are more prone to health problems. Research has even shown that obesity takes years off a dog's life. With that in mind, resist the urge to overfeed and over-treat. Don't make unnecessary additions to your dog's diet, whether with tidbits or with extra vitamins and minerals.

The amount of food needed for proper maintenance will vary

THE DARK SIDE OF CHOCOLATE

From a tiny chip to a giant rabbit, chocolate—in any form—is not your dog's friend. Whether it's an Oreo® cookie, a Snickers® bar or even a couple of M&M's®, you should avoid these items with your dog. You are also well advised to avoid any bone toy that is made out of fake chocolate or any treat made of carob—anything that encourages your dog to become a "chocoholic" can't be helpful. Before you toss your pooch half of your candy bar, consider that as little as a single ounce of chocolate can poison a 30-pound dog. Theobromine, like caffeine, is a methylxanthine and occurs naturally in cocoa beans. Dogs metabolize theobromine very slowly, and its effect on the dog can be serious, harming the heart, kidneys and central nervous system. Dark or semi-sweet chocolate is even worse than milk chocolate, and baking chocolate and cocoa mix are by far the worst.

depending on the individual dog's activity level, but you will be able to tell whether the daily portions are keeping him in good shape. With the wide variety of good complete foods available, choosing what to feed is largely a matter of personal preference. Just as with the puppy, the adult dog should have consistency in his mealtimes (like a morning/evening schedule) and feeding place. In addition to a consistent routine, regular mealtimes also allow the owner to see how much his dog is eating. If the dog seems never to be satisfied or, likewise, becomes uninterested in his food, the owner will know right away that something is wrong and can consult the vet.

DIETS FOR THE AGING DOG

A good rule of thumb is that once a dog has reached 75% of his expected lifespan, he has reached "senior citizen" or geriatric status. Your Bull Terrier will be considered a senior at about 9 years of age; he has a projected lifespan of about 12–15 years.

What does aging have to do with your dog's diet? No, he won't get a discount at the local diner's early-bird special. Yes, he will require some dietary changes to accommodate the changes that come along with increased age. One change is that the older dog's dietary needs become more similar to that of a puppy. Specifically, dogs can metabolize more protein as youngsters and seniors than in the adult-maintenance stage. Discuss with your vet whether you need to switch to a higher-protein or senior-formulated food or whether your current adult-dog food contains sufficient nutrition for the senior.

Watching the dog's weight remains essential, even more so in the senior stage. Older dogs are

Bull Terriers should always have fresh drinking water available from clean bowls.

already more vulnerable to illness, and obesity only contributes to their susceptibility to problems. As the older dog becomes less active and, thus, exercises less, his regular portions may cause him to gain weight. At this point, you may consider decreasing his daily food intake or switching to a reduced-calorie food. As with other changes, you should consult your vet for advice.

WATER

Just as your dog needs proper nutrition from his food, water is an essential "nutrient" as well. Keep plenty of fresh water available for your dog at all times. Remember, the Bull Terrier is

WEIGHT AND SEE!

When you look at yourself in the mirror each day, you get very used to what you see! It's only when you pull out last year's vacation outfit and can't zipper it that you notice that you've put on some pounds. Dog owners are the same way with their dogs. Often a few pounds go unnoticed, and it's not until some time passes or the vet remarks that your dog looks more than pleasantly plump that you realize what's happened. To avoid your pet's becoming obese right under your very nose, make a habit of routinely evaluating his condition with a hands-on test.

Can you feel, but not see, your dog's rib cage? Does your dog have a waist? His waist should be evident by touch and also visible from above and from the side. In top view, the dog's body should have an hourglass shape. These are indicators of good condition.

While it's not hard to spot an extremely skinny or overly rotund dog, it's the subtle changes that lead up to under- or overweight condition of which we must be aware. If your dog's ribs are visible, he is too thin. Conversely, if you can't feel the ribs under too much fat, and if there's no indication of a waistline, your dog is overweight. Both of these conditions require changes to the diet. A trip or sometimes just a call to the vet will help you modify your dog's feeding.

exceptionally active and therefore heats up relatively quickly. The best way to keep him cooled down is to have fresh, cool water always accessible. Water keeps the dog's body properly hydrated and promotes normal function of the body's systems. During housebreaking, it is necessary to keep an eye on how much water your Bull Terrier pup is drinking, but once he is reliably trained, he should have access to clean fresh water at all times. Make sure that the dog's water bowl is clean, and change the water often, making sure that water is always available for your dog, especially if you feed dry food. While we're on the subject, a sturdy steel dish is recommended—plastic or rubber bowls may be eaten by your Bull Terrier.

EXERCISE

The owner of a Bull Terrier well knows the boundless energy of his beloved breed. It should go without saying that the Bull Terrier requires more exercise than your average housedog. A sedentary lifestyle is as harmful to a dog as it is to a person, and when that dog is a Bull Terrier, the routine must be daily! To stay happy, balanced and sane, your Bull Terrier needs ample time to run and play every day. This activity can be divided into two hearty exercise sessions each day, incorporating flying discs, balls

PUPPY STEPS

Puppies are brimming with activity and enthusiasm. It seems that they can play all day and night without tiring, but don't overdo your puppy's exercise regimen. Easy does it for the puppy's first six to nine months. Keep walks brief and don't let the puppy engage in stressful jumping games. The puppy frame is delicate, and too much exercise during those critical growing months can cause injury to his bone structure, ligaments and musculature. Save his first jog for his first birthday!

and anything else you can come up with. Just be sure to keep your Bully under careful supervision!

For those who are more ambitious, you will find that your Bull Terrier also enjoys long walks, an occasional hike or even a swim! Bear in mind that an overweight dog should never be suddenly over-exercised; instead, he should be allowed to increase exercise slowly. Also bear in mind that not only is exercise essential to keep the dog's body fit, it is essential to his mental well-being. A bored dog will find something to do, which often manifests itself in some type of destructive behavior. In this sense, it is essential for the owner's mental well-being as well! Lastly, remember that to ignore a Bull Terrier's exercise needs is tantamount to torture for this very intelligent and active creature. Give him the time and energy he requires and he will reward you ten-thousandfold.

GROOMING

The Bull Terrier's sleek coat does not require fancy grooming or elaborate haircuts. Basically, the

Is there anything a Bull Terrier cannot accomplish? Who can believe this photograph of a Bull Terrier diving into the water on a retrieve. His dexterity and diving style look like those of a well-trained water dog!

Some dog-show exhibitors use groomer's chalk to whiten the white parts of their dogs' coats as part of their grooming routine.

main goal in grooming the Bull Terrier is to keep the dog's coat looking nice and in good health.

Bull Terriers shed their coats twice a year. The dead hair is cast off during these periods, so extra attention should be paid to grooming. A groming glove will help to remove the dead hair and lessen the amount that finds its way onto your carpets, furniture and clothing.

A natural bristle brush or a grooming glove can be used for regular routine brushing. Brushing is effective for removing dead hair and stimulating the dog's natural oils to add shine and a healthy look to the coat. Although the Bull Terrier's coat is short and close, it does require a five-minute once-over every few days to keep it looking its shiny best and to remove dust and debris from the coat. Follow up with a metal comb to remove any hair that remains.

Regular grooming sessions are also a good way to spend time with your dog. Many dogs grow to like the feel of being brushed and will enjoy the hands-on attention.

BATHING

In general, dogs need to be bathed only a few times a year, possibly more often if your dog gets into something messy or if he starts to smell like a dog. Show dogs are usually bathed before every show, which could be as frequent as weekly, although this depends on the owner. Bathing too frequently can have negative effects on the skin and coat, removing natural oils and causing dryness.

If you give your dog his first bath when he is young, he will become accustomed to the process. Wrestling a dog into the tub or chasing a freshly shampooed dog who has escaped from the bath will be no fun! Most dogs don't naturally enjoy their baths, but you at least want your Bull Terrier to cooperate with you.

Before bathing the dog, have the items you'll need close at hand. First, decide where you will bathe the dog. You should have a tub or basin with a non-slip surface. In warm weather, some like to use a portable pool in the yard, although you'll want to make sure your dog doesn't head for the nearest dirt pile following his bath! You will also need a hose or shower spray to wet the coat thoroughly, a shampoo formulated for dogs and several absorbent towels. Human shampoos are too harsh for dogs' coats and will dry them out.

Before wetting the dog, give him a brush-through to remove any dead hair and dirt. Make sure he is at ease in the tub and have the water at a comfortable temperature. Begin bathing by wetting the coat all the way down to the skin. Massage in the shampoo, keeping it away from his face and eyes. Rinse him thoroughly, again avoiding the eyes and ears, as you don't want to get water into the ear canals. A thorough rinsing is important, as shampoo residue is drying and itchy to the dog. After rinsing, wrap him in a towel to absorb the initial moisture and then finish the drying with a fresh dry towel. You should keep the dog indoors and away from drafts until he is completely dry. Only allow him to dry outdoors if it is a warm, sunny day.

NAIL CLIPPING

Having his nails trimmed is not on many dogs' lists of favorite things to do. With this in mind, you will need to accustom your puppy to the procedure at a young age so that he will sit still (well, as still as he can) for his pedicures. Long nails can cause the dog's feet to spread, which is not good for him; likewise, long nails can hurt if they unintentionally scratch, not good for you!

Clean your Bull Terrier's ears regularly with special ear powder or liquid and soft cotton wipes, usually available at your local pet shop.

Some dogs' nails are worn down naturally by regular walking on hard surfaces, so the frequency with which you clip depends on your individual dog. Look at his nails from time to time and clip as

WATER SHORTAGE

No matter how well behaved your dog is, bathing is always a project! Nothing can substitute for a good warm bath, but owners do have the option of giving their dogs "dry" baths. Pet shops sell excellent products, in both powder and spray forms, designed for spot-cleaning your dog. These dry shampoos are convenient for touch-up jobs when you don't have the time to bathe your dog in the traditional way.

Muddy feet, messy behinds and smelly coats can be spot-cleaned and deodorized with a "wet-nap"-style cleaner. On those days when your dog insists on rolling in fresh goose droppings and there's no time for a bath, a spot bath can save the day. These pre-moistened wipes are also handy for other grooming needs like wiping faces, ears and eyes and freshening tails and behinds.

needed; a good way to know when it's time for a trim is if you hear your dog clicking as he walks across the floor.

There are several types of nail clippers and even electric nail-grinding tools made for dogs; first we'll discuss using the clipper. To start, have your clipper ready and some doggie treats on hand. You want your pup to view his nail-clipping sessions in a positive light, and what better way to convince him than with food? You may want to enlist the help of an assistant to comfort the pup and offer treats as you concentrate on the clipping itself. The guillotine-type clipper is thought of by many as the easiest type to use; the nail tip is inserted into the

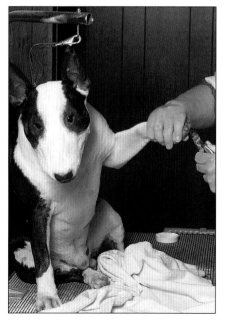

How often your Bull Terrier's nails need clipping will depend upon how much walking on hard surfaces the dog does.

> ### SCOOTING HIS BOTTOM
> Here's a doggy problem that many owners tend to neglect. If your dog is scooting his rear end around the carpet, he probably is experiencing anal-sac impaction or blockage. The anal sacs are the two grape-sized glands on either side of the dog's vent. The dog cannot empty these glands, which become filled with a foul-smelling material. The dog may attempt to lick the area to relieve the pressure. He may also rub his anus on your walls, furniture or floors.
>
> Don't neglect your dog's rear end during grooming sessions. By squeezing both sides of the anus with a soft cloth, you can express some of the material in the sacs. If the material is pasty and thick, you likely will need the assistance of a veterinarian. Vets know how to express the glands and can show you how to do it correctly without hurting the dog or spraying yourself with the unpleasant liquid.

opening, and blades on the top and bottom snip it off in one clip.

Start by grasping the pup's paw; a little pressure on the foot pad causes the nail to extend, making it easier to clip. Clip off a little at a time. If you can see the "quick," which is a blood vessel that runs through each nail, you will know how much to trim, as you do not want to cut into the quick. On that note, if you do cut the quick, which will cause bleeding, you can stem the flow of blood with a styptic pencil or other clotting agent. If you mistakenly nip the quick, do not panic or fuss, as this will cause the pup to be afraid. Simply reassure the pup, stop the bleeding and move on to the next nail. Don't be discouraged; you will become a professional canine pedicurist with practice.

You may or may not be able to see the quick, so it's best to just clip off a small bit at a time. If you see a dark dot in the center of the nail, this is the quick and your cue to stop clipping. Tell the puppy he's a "good boy" and offer a piece of treat with each nail. You can also use nail-clipping

time to examine the footpads, making sure that they are not dry and cracked and that nothing has become embedded in them.

The nail grinder, the second choice, is many owners' first choice. Accustoming the puppy to the sound of the grinder and sensation of the buzz presents fewer challenges than the clipper, and there's no chance of cutting through the quick. Use the grinder on a low setting and always talk soothingly to your dog. He won't mind his salon visit, and he'll have nicely polished nails as well.

Ear Cleaning

While keeping your dog's ears clean unfortunately will not cause

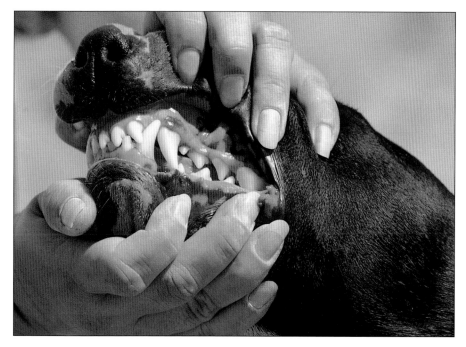

Keep your Bull Terrier's teeth clean and white. Make brushing your dog's teeth with canine dental-care items part of the grooming routine, offer him dental bones and crunchy treats and have an annual veterinary dental exam and cleaning.

him to "hear" your commands any better, it will protect him from ear infection and ear-mite infestation. In addition, a dog's ears are vulnerable to waxy build-up and to collecting foreign matter from the outdoors. Look in your dog's ears regularly to ensure that they look pink, clean and otherwise healthy. Even if they look fine, an odor in the ears signals a problem and means it's time to call the vet.

A dog's ears should be cleaned regularly; once a week is suggested, and you can do this along with your regular brushing. Using a cotton ball or pad, and never probing into the ear canal, wipe the ear gently. You can use an ear-cleansing liquid or powder available from your veterinarian or pet-supply store; alternatively, you might prefer to use home-made solutions with ingredients like one part white vinegar and one part hydrogen peroxide. Ask your veterinarian about home remedies before you attempt to concoct something on your own!

Keep your Bull Terrier's ears free of excess hair by plucking it as needed. If done gently, this will be painless for the dog. Look for wax, brown droppings (a sign of ear mites), redness or any other abnormalities. At the first sign of a problem, contact your veterinarian so that he can prescribe an appropriate medication.

EYE CARE

During grooming sessions, pay extra attention to the condition of your dog's eyes. If the area around the eyes is soiled or if tear staining has occurred, there are various cleaning agents made especially for this purpose. Look at the dog's eyes to make sure no debris has entered; dogs with large eyes and those who spend time outdoors are especially prone to this.

The signs of an eye infection are obvious: mucus, redness, puffiness, scabs or other signs of irritation. If your dog's eyes become infected, the vet will likely prescribe an antibiotic ointment for treatment. If you notice signs of more serious problems, such as opacities in the eye, which usually indicate cataracts, consult the vet at once. Taking time to pay attention to your dog's eyes will alert you in the early stages of any problem so that you can get your dog treatment as soon as possible. You could save your dog's sight!

IDENTIFICATION AND TRAVEL

ID FOR YOUR DOG

You love your Bull Terrier and want to keep him safe. Of course, you take every precaution to prevent his escaping from the yard or becoming lost or stolen. You have a sturdy high fence and you always keep your dog on lead when out and about in public places. If your dog is not properly identified, however, you are overlooking a major aspect of his safety. We hope to never be in a situation where our dog is missing, but we should practice prevention in the unfortunate case that this happens; identification greatly increases the chances of your dog's being returned to you

There are several ways to identify your dog. First, the traditional dog tag should be a staple in your dog's wardrobe, attached to his everyday collar. Tags can be made of sturdy plastic and various metals and should include your contact information so that a person who finds the dog can get in touch with you right away to arrange his return. Many people today enjoy the wide range of decorative tags available, so have fun and create a tag to match your dog's personality. Of course, it is important that the tag stays on the collar, so have a secure "O" ring attachment; you also can explore the type of tag that slides right onto the collar.

In addition to the ID tag, which every dog should wear even if identified by another method, two other forms of identification have become popular: microchipping and tattooing. In microchipping, a tiny scannable chip is painlessly inserted under the dog's skin. The number is registered to you so that, if your lost dog turns up at a clinic or shelter, the chip can be scanned to retrieve your contact information.

The advantage of the microchip is that it is a permanent form of ID, but there are some factors to consider. Several different companies make microchips, and not all are compatible with the others' scanning devices. It's best to find a company with a universal microchip that can be read by scanners made by other companies as well. It won't do any good to have the dog chipped if the information cannot be retrieved. Also, not every humane society, shelter and clinic is equipped with a scanner, although more and more facilities are equipping themselves. In fact,

PET OR STRAY?

Besides the obvious benefit of providing your contact information to whoever finds your lost dog, an ID tag makes your dog more approachable and more likely to be recovered. A strange dog wandering the neighborhood without a collar and tags will look like a stray, while the collar and tags indicate that the dog is someone's pet. Even if the ID tags become detached from the collar, the collar alone will make a person more likely to pick up the dog.

many shelters microchip dogs that they adopt out to new homes.

Because the microchip is not visible to the eye, the dog must wear a tag that states that he is microchipped so that whoever picks him up will know to have him scanned. He of course also should have a tag with contact information in case his chip cannot be read. Humane societies and veterinary clinics offer microchipping service, which is usually very affordable.

Though less popular than microchipping, tattooing is another permanent method of ID for dogs. Most vets perform this service, and there are also clinics that perform dog tattooing. This is also an affordable procedure and one that will not cause much discomfort for the dog. It is best to put the tattoo in a visible area, such as the ear, to deter theft. It is sad to say that there are cases of dogs' being stolen and sold to research laboratories, but such laboratories will not accept tattooed dogs.

To ensure that the tattoo is effective in aiding your dog's return to you, the tattoo number must be registered with a national organization. That way, when someone finds a tattooed dog, a phone call to the registry will quickly match the dog with his owner.

HIT THE ROAD

Car travel with your Bull Terrier may be limited to necessity only, such as trips to the vet, or you may bring your dog along almost everywhere you go. This will depend much on your individual dog and how he reacts to rides in the car. You can begin desensitizing your dog to car travel as a pup so that it's something that he's used to. Still, some dogs suffer from motion sickness. Your vet may prescribe a medication for this if trips in the car pose a problem for your dog. At the very least, you will need to get him to the vet, so he will need to tolerate these trips with the least amount of hassle possible.

Start taking your pup on short trips, maybe just around the block

CAN I COME, TOO?

Your dog can accompany you most anywhere you go. A picnic in the park and the kids' Little League game are just two examples of outdoor events where dogs likely will be welcome. Of course, your dog will need to be kept on lead or safely crated in a well-ventilated crate. Bring along your "doggie bag" with all of the supplies you will need, like water, food or treats and a stash of plastic bags or other clean-up aids. Including your dog in the family activities is fun for all of you, providing excellent owner/dog quality time and new socialization opportunities.

Bring along what you will need for the dog. He should wear his collar and ID tags, of course, and you should bring his leash, water (and food if a long trip) and clean-up materials for potty breaks and in case of motion sickness. Always keep your dog on his leash when you make stops, and never leave him alone in the car. Many a dog has died from the heat inside a closed car; this does not take much time at all in any kind of weather. A dog left alone inside a car can also be a target for thieves.

to start. If he is fine with short trips, lengthen your rides a little at a time. Start to take him on your errands or just for drives around town. By this time it will be easy to tell whether your dog is a born traveler or would prefer staying at home when you are on the road.

Of course, safety is a concern for dogs in the car. First, he must travel securely, not left loose to roam about the car where he could be injured or distract the driver. A young pup can be held by a passenger initially but should soon graduate to a travel crate, which can be the same crate he uses in the home. Other options include a car harness (like a seat belt for dogs) and partitioning the back of the car with a gate made for this purpose.

A family vacation with the Bull Terrier will surely include a day near the water.

BASIC TRAINING PRINCIPLES: PUPPY VS. ADULT

There's a big difference between training an adult dog and training a young puppy. With a young puppy, everything is new. At eight to ten weeks of age, he will be experiencing many things, and he has nothing with which to compare these experiences. Up to this point, he has been with his dam and littermates, not one-on-one with people except in his interactions with his breeder and visitors to the litter.

When you first bring the puppy home, he is eager to please you. This means that he accepts doing things your way. During the next couple of months, he will absorb the basis of everything he needs to know for the rest of his life. This early age is even referred to as the "sponge" stage. After that, for the next 18 months, it's up to you to reinforce good manners by building on the foundation that you've established. Once your puppy is reliable in basic commands and behavior and has reached the appropriate age, you may gradually introduce him to some of the interesting sports, games and activities available to pet owners and their dogs.

Raising your puppy is a family affair. Each member of the family must know what rules to set forth for the puppy and how to use the same one-word commands to mean exactly the same thing every time. Even if yours is a large family, one person will soon be considered by the pup to be the leader, the Alpha person in his pack, the "boss" who must be obeyed. Often that highly regarded person turns out to be the one who feeds the puppy. Food ranks very high on the puppy's list of important things! That's why your puppy is rewarded with small treats along with verbal praise when he responds to you correctly. As the

LEADER OF THE PACK

Canines are pack animals. They live according to pack rules, and every pack has only one leader. Guess what? That's you! To establish your position of authority, lay down the rules and be fair and good-natured in all your dealings with your dog. He will consider young children as his littermates, but the one who trains him, who feeds him, who grooms him, who expects him to come into line, that's his leader. And he who leads must be obeyed.

puppy learns to do what you want him to do, the food rewards are gradually eliminated and only the praise remains. If you were to keep up with the food treats, you could have two problems on your hands—an obese dog and a beggar.

Training begins the minute your Bull Terrier puppy steps through the doorway of your home, so don't make the mistake of putting the puppy on the floor and telling him by your actions to "Go for it! Run wild!" Even if this is your first puppy, you must act as if you know what you're doing: be the boss. An uncertain pup may be terrified to move, while a bold one will be ready to take you at your word and start plotting to destroy the house! Before you collected your puppy, you decided where his own special place would be, and that's where to put him when you first arrive home. Give him a house tour after he has investigated his area and had a nap and a bathroom "pit stop."

It's worth mentioning here that, if you've adopted an adult dog that is completely trained to your liking, lucky you! You're off the hook! However, if that dog spent his life up to this point in a kennel, or even in a good home but without any real training, be prepared to tackle the job ahead. A dog three years of age or older with no previous training cannot

be blamed for not knowing what he was never taught. While the dog is trying to understand and learn your rules, at the same time he has to unlearn many of his previously self-taught habits and general view of the world.

Working with a professional trainer will speed up your progress with an adopted adult dog. You'll need patience, too. Some new rules may be close to impossible for the dog to accept. After all, he's been successful so far by doing everything his way! (Patience again.) He may agree with your instruction for a few

At 12 weeks of age, this young lady is looking up to her new pack to provide her with safety and guidance.

days and then slip back into his old ways, so you must be just as consistent and understanding in your teaching as you would be with a puppy. (More patience needed yet again!) Your dog has to learn to pay attention to your voice, your family, the daily routine, new smells, new sounds and, in some cases, even a new climate.

One of the most important things to find out about a newly adopted adult dog is his reaction to children (yours and others), strangers and your friends, and how he acts upon meeting other dogs. If he was not socialized with dogs as a puppy, this could be a major problem. This does not mean that he's a "bad" dog, a vicious dog or an aggressive dog; rather, it means that he has no idea how to read another dog's body language. There's no way for him to tell whether the other dog is a friend or foe. Survival instinct takes over, telling him to attack first and ask questions later. This definitely calls for professional help and, even then, may not be a behavior that can be corrected 100% reliably (or even at all). If you have a puppy, this is why it is so very important to introduce your young puppy properly to other puppies and "dog-friendly" adult dogs.

Your Bull Terrier may in fact challenge your dominance and try to take over as leader of the pack. This is a dog who likes to rule the roost! However, you must be the one in charge, and you must assert your authority. Firm corrections and consistency will keep your Bull Terrier in line. Remember that harsh corrections and physical discipline is never suitable; be firm but fair.

Basic obedience training for your Bull Terrier is absolutely essential. Proper training provides not only good manners for your Bull Terrier but also emotional stability and socialization. Because Bull Terriers were bred for strong prey behaviors and less for pack instincts, they generally respond best to training when motivated with food and toys. The Bull Terrier must be handled firmly but with patience and lots of positive reinforcement. Young Bull Terriers can be very rambunctious and must be taught

Your pup's first taste of "pack rules" came in the form of posturing for position in the litter with his siblings—a longstanding canine ritual yet all in good fun!

An important aspect of training is bonding with your dog. The more your Bull Terrier trusts you, the more he will want to please you.

not to jump or nip and grab when playing with small children or elderly people.

The dog's owner is the best trainer for a Bull Terrier. You and your Bully will do well in obedience classes that you attend

together, but you should never send your dog off to learn from a trainer with no participation from you. A big part of dog/owner training is the bond that is formed, laying the foundation for a relationship of mutual respect and trust. Just have patience! Training a Bully can be a challenge. This intelligent dog will often find a million things more interesting than the lesson at hand, so don't push his attention span. Keep lessons happy and short before the dog loses focus and your efforts become futile.

HOUSE-TRAINING YOUR BULL TERRIER

Dogs are tactility-oriented when it comes to house-training. In other words, they respond to the surface on which they are given approval

---

I WILL FOLLOW YOU

Obedience isn't just a classroom activity. In your home you have many great opportunities to teach your dog polite manners. Allowing your pet on the bed or furniture elevates him to your level, which is not a good idea (the word is "Off!"). Use the "umbilical cord" method, keeping your dog on lead so he has to go with you wherever you go. You sit, he sits. You walk, he heels. You stop, he sit-stays. Everywhere you go, he's with you, but you go first!

to eliminate. The choice is yours (the dog's version is in parentheses): The lawn (including the neighbors' lawns)? A bare patch of earth under a tree (where people like to sit and relax in the summertime)? Concrete steps or patio (all sidewalks, garages and basement floors)? The curbside (watch out for cars)? A small area of crushed stone in a corner of the yard (mine!)? The latter is the best choice if you can manage it, because it will remain strictly for the dog's use and is easy to keep clean.

You can start out with paper-training indoors and switch over to an outdoor surface as the puppy matures and gains control over his need to eliminate. For the nay-sayers, don't worry—this won't mean that the dog will soil on every piece of newspaper lying around the house. You are training him to go outside, remember? Starting out by paper-training often is the only choice for a city dog.

WHEN YOUR PUPPY'S "GOT TO GO"
Your puppy's need to relieve himself is seemingly non-stop, but signs of improvement will be seen each week. From 8 to 10 weeks old, the puppy will have to be taken outside every time he wakes

DAILY SCHEDULE

How many relief trips does your puppy need per day? A puppy up to the age of 14 weeks will need to go outside about 8 to 12 times per day! You will have to take the pup out any time he starts sniffing around the floor or turning in small circles, as well as after naps, meals, games and lessons or whenever he's released from his crate. Once the puppy is 14 to 22 weeks of age, he will require only 6 to 8 relief trips. At the ages of 22 to 32 weeks, the puppy will require about 5 to 7 trips. Adult dogs typically require 4 relief trips per day, in the morning, afternoon, evening and late at night.

up, about 10–15 minutes after every meal and after every period of play—all day long, from first thing in the morning until his bedtime! That's a total of ten or more trips per day to teach the puppy where it's okay to relieve himself. With that schedule in mind, you can see that house-training a young puppy is not a part-time job. It requires someone to be home all day.

If that seems overwhelming or impossible, do a little planning. For example, plan to pick up your

An adult Bull Terrier will only need to have bowel movements about twice per day, depending on feeding schedule and exercise.

puppy at the start of a vacation period. If you can't get home in the middle of the day, plan to hire a dog-sitter or ask a neighbor to come over to take the pup outside, feed him his lunch and then take him out again about ten or so minutes after he's eaten. Also make arrangements with that or another person to be your "emergency" contact if you have to stay late on the job. Remind yourself—repeatedly—that this hectic schedule improves as the puppy gets older.

HOME WITHIN A HOME

Your Bull Terrier puppy needs to be confined to one secure, puppy-proof area when no one is able to watch his every move. Generally the kitchen is the place of choice because the floor is washable. Likewise, it's a busy family area that will accustom the pup to a

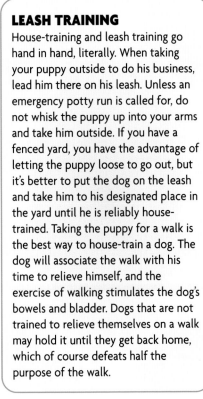

LEASH TRAINING

House-training and leash training go hand in hand, literally. When taking your puppy outside to do his business, lead him there on his leash. Unless an emergency potty run is called for, do not whisk the puppy up into your arms and take him outside. If you have a fenced yard, you have the advantage of letting the puppy loose to go out, but it's better to put the dog on the leash and take him to his designated place in the yard until he is reliably house-trained. Taking the puppy for a walk is the best way to house-train a dog. The dog will associate the walk with his time to relieve himself, and the exercise of walking stimulates the dog's bowels and bladder. Dogs that are not trained to relieve themselves on a walk may hold it until they get back home, which of course defeats half the purpose of the walk.

POTTY COMMAND

Most dogs love to please their masters; there are no bounds to what dogs will do to make their owners happy. The potty command is a good example of this theory. If toileting on command makes the master happy, then more power to him. Puppies will obligingly piddle if it really makes their keepers smile. Some owners can be creative about which word they will use to command their dogs to relieve themselves. Some popular choices are "Potty," "Tinkle," "Piddle," "Let's go," "Hurry up" and "Toilet." Give the command every time your puppy goes into position and the puppy will begin to associate his business with the command.

variety of noises, everything from pots and pans to the telephone, blender and dishwasher. He will also be enchanted by the smell of your cooking (and will never be critical when you burn something). An exercise pen (also called an "ex-pen," a puppy version of a playpen) within the room of choice is an excellent

means of confinement for a young pup. He can see out and has a certain amount of space in which to run about, but he is safe from dangerous things like electrical cords, heating units, trash baskets or open kitchen-supply cabinets. Place the pen where the puppy will not get a blast of heat or air conditioning.

In the pen, you can put a few toys, his bed (which can be his crate if the dimensions of pen and crate are compatible) and a few layers of newspaper in one small corner, just in case. A water bowl can be hung at a convenient height on the side of the ex-pen so it won't become a splashing pool for an innovative puppy. His food dish can go on the floor, near but not under the water bowl.

Every Bull Terrier should have his own crate. Crate training can be extremely useful to the Bull Terrier owner and the crate can be a haven for your Bull Terrier. If you leave a crate in your house, with the door open, and your Bull Terrier is temporarily "missing," you will probably find him in his crate—*resting*!

Crates are something that pet owners are at last getting used to for their dogs. Wild or domestic canines have always preferred to sleep in den-like safe spots, and that is exactly what the crate provides. How often have you seen adult dogs that choose to sleep under a table or chair even

CANINE DEVELOPMENT SCHEDULE

It is important to understand how and at what age a puppy develops into adulthood.
If you are a puppy owner, consult the following Canine Development Schedule to
determine the stage of development your puppy is currently experiencing.
This knowledge will help you as you work with the puppy in the weeks and months ahead.

PERIOD	AGE	CHARACTERISTICS
FIRST TO THIRD	BIRTH TO SEVEN WEEKS	Puppy needs food, sleep and warmth and responds to simple and gentle touching. Needs mother for security and disciplining. Needs littermates for learning and interacting with other dogs. Pup learns to function within a pack and learns pack order of dominance. Begin socializing pup with adults and children for short periods. Pup begins to become aware of his environment.
FOURTH	EIGHT TO TWELVE WEEKS	Brain is fully developed. Pup needs socializing with outside world. Remove from mother and littermates. Needs to change from canine pack to human pack. Human dominance necessary. Fear period occurs between 8 and 12 weeks. Avoid fright and pain.
FIFTH	THIRTEEN TO SIXTEEN WEEKS	Training and formal obedience should begin. Less association with other dogs, more with people, places, situations. Period will pass easily if you remember this is pup's change-to-adolescence time. Be firm and fair. Flight instinct prominent. Permissiveness and over-disciplining can do permanent damage. Praise for good behavior.
JUVENILE	FOUR TO EIGHT MONTHS	Another fear period about 7 to 8 months of age. It passes quickly, but be cautious of fright and pain. Sexual maturity reached. Dominant traits established. Dog should understand sit, down, come and stay by now.

NOTE: THESE ARE APPROXIMATE TIME FRAMES. ALLOW FOR INDIVIDUAL DIFFERENCES IN PUPPIES.

This is what we call the "denning instinct"!

though they have full run of the house? It's the den connection.

In your "happy" voice, use the word "Crate" every time you put the pup into his den. If he's new to a crate, toss in a small biscuit for him to chase the first few times. At night, after he's been outside, he should sleep in his crate. The crate may be kept in his designated area at night or, if you want to be sure to hear those wake-up yips in the morning, put the crate in a corner of your bedroom. However, don't make any response whatsoever to whining or crying. If he's completely ignored, he'll settle down and get to sleep.

Good bedding for a young puppy is an old folded bath towel or an old blanket, something that is easily washable and disposable if necessary ("accidents" will happen!). Never put newspaper in the puppy's crate. Also those old ideas about adding a clock to replace his mother's heartbeat, or a hot-water bottle to replace her

warmth, are just that—old ideas. The clock could drive the puppy nuts, and the hot-water bottle could end up as a very soggy waterbed! An extremely good breeder would have introduced your puppy to the crate by letting two pups sleep together for a couple of nights, followed by several nights alone. How thankful you will be if you found that breeder!

Safe toys in the pup's crate or area will keep him occupied, but monitor their condition closely. Discard any toys that show signs of being chewed to bits. Squeaky parts, bits of stuffing or plastic or

EXTRA! EXTRA!
The headlines read: "Puppy Piddles Here!" Breeders commonly use newspapers to line their whelping pens, so puppies learn to associate newspapers with relieving themselves. Do not use newspapers to line your pup's crate, as this will signal to your puppy that it is OK to urinate in his crate. If you choose to paper-train your puppy, you will layer newspapers on a section of the floor near the door he uses to go outside. You should encourage the puppy to use the papers to relieve himself, and bring him there whenever you see him getting ready to go. Little by little, you will reduce the size of the newspaper-covered area so that the puppy will learn to relieve himself "on the other side of the door."

any other small pieces can cause intestinal blockage or possibly choking if swallowed, which is why it's best to purchase only the sturdiest toys designed for strong chewers.

You can gradually increase the time he is left alone to get him used to it. The pet crate is comfortable to your Bull Terrier because, like his wild ancestors, he instinctively seeks the safety and security of a "den." The fact that we may see the crate as a very limited space, or very confining is only a human view. Both puppies and adult dogs can be placed in their crates when their owners are away from home for several hours. They also do not mind being placed in a crate for the night (when they haven't wormed their way into your bed) and you will have peace of mind knowing your dog is safe.

PROGRESSING WITH POTTY-TRAINING

After you've taken your puppy out and he has relieved himself in the area you've selected, he can have some free time with the family as long as there is someone responsible for watching him. That doesn't mean just someone in the same room who is watching TV or busy on the computer, but one person who is doing nothing other than keeping an eye on the pup, playing with him on the floor and helping him understand his position in the pack.

SOMEBODY TO BLAME

House-training a puppy can be frustrating for the puppy and the owner alike. The puppy does not instinctively understand the difference between defecating on the pavement outside and on the ceramic tile in the kitchen. He is confused and frightened by his human's exuberant reactions to his natural urges. The owner, arguably the more intelligent of the duo, is also frustrated that he cannot convince his puppy to obey his commands and instructions.

In frustration, the owner may struggle with the temptation to discipline the puppy, scold him or even strike him on the rear end. Harsh corrections are completely inappropriate, and will defeat your purpose in gaining your puppy's trust and respect. Don't blame your nine-week-old puppy. Blame yourself for not being 100% consistent in the puppy's lessons and routine. The lesson here is simple: try harder and your puppy will succeed.

This first taste of freedom will let you begin to set the house rules. If you don't want the dog on the furniture, now is the time to prevent his first attempts to jump up onto the couch. The word to use in this case is "Off," not "Down." "Down" is the word you will use to teach the down position, which is something entirely different.

Most corrections at this stage come in the form of simply distracting the puppy. Instead of telling him "No" for "Don't chew the carpet," distract the chomping puppy with a toy and he'll forget about the carpet.

As you are playing with the pup, do not forget to watch him closely and pay attention to his body language. Whenever you see him begin to circle or sniff, take the puppy outside to relieve himself. If you are paper-training, put him back into his confined area on the newspapers. In either case, praise him as he eliminates while he actually is in the act of relieving himself. Three seconds after he has finished is too late! You'll be praising him for running toward you, or picking up a toy or whatever he may be doing at that moment, and that's not what you want to be praising him for. Timing is a vital tool in all dog training. Use it.

Remove soiled newspapers immediately and replace them with clean ones. You may want to take a small piece of soiled paper and place it in the middle of the new clean papers, as the scent will attract him to that spot when it's time to go again. That scent attraction is why it's so important to clean up any messes made in the house by using a product specially made to eliminate the odor of dog urine and droppings. Regular household cleansers won't do the trick. Pet shops sell the best pet deodorizers. Invest in the largest container you can find.

Scent attraction eventually will lead your pup to his chosen spot outdoors; this is the basis of outdoor training. When you take your puppy outside to relieve himself, use a one-word command such as "Outside" or "Go-potty" (that's one word to the puppy!) as you pick him up and attach his leash. Then put him down in his area. If for any reason you can't carry him, snap the leash on quickly and lead him to his spot. Now comes the hard part—hard for you, that is. Just stand there until he urinates and defecates. Move him a few feet in one direction or another if he's just sitting there looking at you, but remember that this is neither

---

BASIC PRINCIPLES OF DOG TRAINING

1. Start training early. A young puppy is ready, willing and able.
2. Timing is your all-important tool. Praise at the exact time that the dog responds correctly. Pay close attention.
3. Patience is almost as important as timing!
4. Repeat! The same word has to mean the same thing every time.
5. In the beginning, praise all correct behavior verbally, along with treats and petting.

Dogs learn by watching. Bull Terriers are as playful and energetic as they are perceptive and intelligent.

playtime nor time for a walk. This is strictly a business trip! Then, as he circles and squats (remember your timing!), give him a quiet "Good dog" as praise. If you start to jump for joy, ecstatic over his performance, he'll do one of two things: either he will stop midstream, as it were, or he'll do it again for you—in the house—and expect you to be just as delighted!

Give him five minutes or so and, if he doesn't go in that time, take him back indoors to his confined area and try again in another ten minutes, or immediately if you see him sniffing and circling. By careful observation, you'll soon work out a successful schedule.

Accidents, by the way, are just that—accidents. Clean them up quickly and thoroughly, without comment, after the puppy has been taken outside to finish his business and then put back into his area or crate. If you witness an accident in progress, say "No!" in a stern voice and get the pup outdoors immediately. No punishment is needed. You and your puppy are just learning each other's language, and sometimes it's easy to miss a puppy's message. Chalk it up to experience and watch more closely from now on.

KEEPING THE PACK ORDERLY

Discipline is a form of training that brings order to life. For example, military discipline is what allows the soldiers in an army to work as one. Discipline is a form of teaching and, in dogs, is the basis of how the successful pack operates. Each member knows his place in the pack and

Once you have earned your Bull Terrier's love and trust, you have a friend that will follow you to the ends of the earth! Now that's something to get happy about!

social coexistence that all canines recognize and accept. Discipline, therefore, is never to be confused with punishment. When you teach your puppy how you want him to behave, and he behaves properly and you praise him for it, you are disciplining him with a form of positive reinforcement.

For a dog, rewards come in the form of praise, a smile, a cheerful tone of voice, a few friendly pats or a rub of the ears. Rewards are also small food treats. Obviously, that does not mean bits of regular dog food. Instead, treats are very small bits of special things like cheese or pieces of soft dog treats. The idea is to reward the dog with something very small that he can taste and swallow, providing instant positive reinforcement. If he has to take time to chew the treat, he will have forgotten what he did to earn it by the time he is finished!

all respect the leader, or Alpha dog. It is essential for your puppy that you establish this type of relationship, with you as the Alpha, or leader. It is a form of

Your puppy should never be physically punished. The displeasure shown on your face and in your voice is sufficient to signal to the pup that he has done something wrong. He wants to please everyone higher up on the social ladder, especially his leader, so a scowl and harsh voice will take care of the error. Growling out the word "Shame!" when the pup is caught in the act of doing something wrong is better than the repetitive "No."

SHOULD WE ENROLL?

If you have the means and the time, you should definitely take your dog to obedience classes. Begin with Puppy Kindergarten Classes in which puppies of all sizes learn basic lessons while getting the opportunity to meet and greet each other; it's as much about socialization as it is about good manners. What you learn in class you can practice at home. And if you goof up in practice, you'll get help in the next session.

Some dogs hear "No" so often that they begin to think it's their name! By the way, do not use the dog's name when you're correcting him. His name is reserved to get his attention for something pleasant about to take place.

There are punishments that have nothing to do with you. For example, your dog may think that chasing cats is one reason for his existence. You can try to stop it as much as you like but without success, because it's such fun for the dog. But one good hissing, spitting swipe of a cat's claws across the dog's nose will put an end to the game forever. Intervene only when your dog's eyeball is seriously at risk. Cat scratches can cause permanent damage to an innocent but annoying puppy.

An amazingly athletic feat for a dog of her inches! This Bull Terrier bitch epitomizes the energy and athleticism of the breed.

PUPPY KINDERGARTEN

COLLAR AND LEASH

Before you begin your Bull Terrier puppy's education, he must be used to his collar and leash. Choose a collar for your puppy that is secure, but not heavy or bulky. He won't enjoy training if he's uncomfortable. A flat buckle collar is fine for everyday wear and for initial puppy training. For older dogs, there are several types of training collars such as the martingale, which is a double loop that tightens slightly around the neck, or the head collar, which is similar to a horse's halter.

A chain choke collar can be an effective tool in training your adult (*not* puppy) Bull Terrier if you know how to use it. Some breeders recommend using a choke collar for daily walks, as the Bully is a strong breed with a tendency to pull. He can slip out of a traditional collar easily, and

---

WHO'S TRAINING WHOM?

Dog training is a black-and-white exercise. The correct response to a command must be absolute, and the trainer must insist on completely accurate responses from the dog. A trainer cannot command his dog to sit and then settle for the dog's melting into the down position. Often owners are so pleased that their dogs "did something" in response to a command that they just shrug and say, "OK, Down" even though they wanted the dog to sit. You want your dog to respond to the command without hesitation: he must respond at that moment and correctly every time.

Bull Terriers require heavy-duty collars. Remember, this is a strong breed!

the choke collar is helpful in controlling a determined puller. It releases when the dog stops pulling; in this way, the dog will learn that it's much more comfortable to walk at your pace. Of course, a sturdy leash is needed no matter what type of collar or harness is used.

A lightweight 6-foot woven cotton or nylon training leash is preferred by most trainers because it is easy to fold up in your hand and comfortable to hold because there is a certain amount of give to it. There are lessons where the dog will start off 6 feet away from you at the end of the leash. The leash used to take the puppy outside to relieve himself is shorter because you don't want him to roam away from his area. The shorter leash will also be the one to use when you walk the puppy.

If you've been wise enough to enroll in a Puppy Kindergarten training class, suggestions will be made as to the best collar and leash for your young puppy. I say "wise" because your puppy will be in a class with puppies in his age range (up to five months old) of all breeds and sizes. It's the perfect way for him to learn the right way (and the wrong way) to interact with other dogs as well as their people. You cannot teach your puppy how to interpret another dog's sign language. For a first-time puppy owner, these socialization classes are invaluable. For experienced dog owners, they are a real boon to further training.

ATTENTION
You've been using the dog's name since the minute you collected him from the breeder, so you should be able to get his attention by saying his name—with a big

BE UPSTANDING!
You are the dog's leader. During training, stand up straight so your dog looks up at you, and therefore up *to* you. Say the command words distinctly, in a clear, declarative tone of voice. (No barking!) Give rewards only as the correct response takes place (remember your timing!). Praise, smiles and treats are "rewards" used to positively reinforce correct responses. Don't repeat a mistake. Just change to another exercise—you will soon find success!

smile and in an excited tone of voice. His response will be the puppy equivalent of "Here I am! What are we going to do?" Your immediate response (if you haven't guessed by now) is "Good dog." Rewarding him at the moment he pays attention to you teaches him the proper way to respond when he hears his name.

EXERCISES FOR A BASIC CANINE EDUCATION

THE SIT EXERCISE

There are several ways to teach the puppy to sit. The first one is to catch him whenever he is about to sit and, as his backside nears the floor, say "Sit, good dog!" That's positive reinforcement and, if your timing is sharp, he will learn that what he's doing at that second is connected to your saying "Sit" and that you think he's clever for doing it!

Another method is to start with the puppy on his leash in front of you. Show him a treat in the palm of your right hand. Bring your hand up under his nose and, almost in slow motion, move your hand up and back so his nose goes up in the air and his head tilts back as he follows the treat in your hand. At that point, he will have to either sit or fall over, so as his back legs buckle under, say "Sit, good dog," and then give him the treat and lots of praise. You may have to begin with your

hand lightly running up his chest, actually lifting his chin up until he sits. Some (usually older) dogs require gentle pressure on their hindquarters with the left hand, in which case the dog should be on your left side. Puppies generally do not appreciate this physical dominance.

After a few times, you should be able to show the dog a treat in the open palm of your hand, raise

READY, SIT, GO!

On your marks, get set: train! Most professional trainers agree that the sit command is the place to start your dog's formal education. Sitting is a natural posture for most dogs, and they respond to the sit exercise willingly and readily. For every lesson, begin with the sit command so that you start out on a successful note; likewise, you should practice the sit command at the end of every lesson as well, because you always want to end on a high note.

A SIMPLE "SIT"

When you command your dog to sit, use the word "Sit." Do not say "Sit down," as your dog will not know whether you mean "Sit" or "Down," or maybe you mean both. Be clear in your instructions to your dog; use one-word commands and always be consistent.

Don't save any of these drills only for training sessions. Use them as much as possible at odd times during a normal day. The dog should always sit before being given his food dish. He should sit to let you go through a doorway first, when the doorbell rings or when you stop to speak to someone on the street.

THE DOWN EXERCISE

Before beginning to teach the down command, you must consider how the dog feels about this exercise. To him, "down" is a submissive position. Being flat on the floor with you standing over him is not his idea of fun. It's up to you to let him know that, while it may not be fun, the reward of your approval is worth his effort.

Start with the puppy on your left side in a sit position. Hold the leash right above his collar in your left hand. Have an extra-special treat, such as a small piece of cooked chicken or hot dog, in

Taking a break from the down position, this Bully's chosen reward is a belly rub!

your hand waist-high as you say "Sit" and have him sit. You will thereby have taught him two things at the same time. Both the verbal command and the motion of the hand are signals for the sit. Your puppy is watching you almost more than he is listening to you, so what you do is just as important as what you say.

your right hand. Place it at the end of the pup's nose and steadily move your hand down and forward along the ground. Hold the leash to prevent a sudden lunge for the food. As the puppy goes into the down position, say "Down" very gently.

The difficulty with this exercise is twofold: it's both the submissive aspect and the fact that most people say the word "Down" as if they were a drill sergeant in charge of recruits! So issue the command sweetly, give him the treat and have the pup maintain the down position for several seconds. If he tries to get up immediately, place your hands on his shoulders and press down gently, giving him a very quiet "Good dog." As you progress with this lesson, increase the "down time" until he will hold it until you say "Okay" (his cue for release). Practice this one in the

OKAY!

This is the signal that tells your dog that he can quit whatever he was doing. Use "Okay" to end a session on a correct response to a command. (Never end on an incorrect response.) Lots of praise follows. People use "Okay" a lot and it has other uses for dogs, too. Your dog is barking. You say, "Okay! Come!" "Okay" signals him to stop the barking activity and "Come" allows him to come to you for a "Good dog."

house at various times throughout the day.

By increasing the length of time during which the dog must maintain the down position, you'll find many uses for it. For example, he can lie at your feet in the vet's office or anywhere that

If you plan to exhibit your Bull Terrier at shows, you'll need to teach and practice the "stand" command.

Your Bull Terrier will heed your commands if you approach training with patience and consistency. The stay command is every photographer's favorite tool.

both of you have to wait, when you are on the phone, while the family is eating and so forth. If you progress to training for competitive obedience, he'll already be all set for the exercise called the "long down."

THE STAY EXERCISE

You can teach your Bull Terrier to stay in the sit, down and stand positions. To teach the sit/stay, have the dog sit on your left side. Hold the leash at waist level in your left hand and let the dog know that you have a treat in your closed right hand. Step forward on your right foot as you say "Stay." Immediately turn and stand directly in front of the dog, keeping your right hand up high so he'll keep his eye on the treat hand and maintain the sit position for a count of five. Return

Once your Bull Terrier understands and obeys a command (such as the stay command), you can vary the location in which you practice.

to your original position and offer the reward.

Increase the length of the sit/stay each time until the dog can hold it for at least 30 seconds without moving. After about a week of success, move out on

you do get frustrated, never let your puppy know! Always keep a positive, upbeat attitude during training, which will transmit to your dog for positive results.

The down/stay is taught in the same way once the dog is completely reliable and steady with the down command. Again, don't rush it. With the dog in the down position on your left side, step out on your right foot as you say "Stay." Return by walking around in back of the dog and into your original position. While you are training, it's okay to murmur something like "Hold on" to encourage him to stay put. When the dog will stay without moving when you are at a distance of 3 or 4 feet, begin to increase the length of time before

The basic commands, such as down/stay, are utilized in agility competition. Between certain obstacles, the dog is required to jump onto a platform and stay for 30 to 60 seconds.

your right foot and take two steps before turning to face the dog. Give the "Stay" hand signal (left palm back toward the dog's head) as you leave. He gets the treat when you return and he holds the sit/stay. Increase the distance that you walk away from him before turning until you reach the length of your training leash. But don't rush it! Go back to the beginning if he moves before he should. No matter what the lesson, never be upset by having to back up for a few days. The repetition and practice are what will make your dog reliable in these commands. It won't do any good to move on to something more difficult if the command is not mastered at the easier levels. Above all, even if

SMILE WHEN YOU ORDER ME AROUND!

While trainers recommend practicing with your dog every day, it's perfectly acceptable to take a "mental health day" off. It's better not to train the dog on days when you're in a sour mood. Your bad attitude or lack of interest will be sensed by your dog, and he will respond accordingly. Studies show that dogs are well tuned in to their humans' emotions. Be conscious of how you use your voice when talking to your dog. Raising your voice or shouting will only erode your dog's trust in you as his trainer and master.

When the family takes off in a car, boat or plane, don't forget your Bull Terrier! He will always want to come along to be with his beloved family.

you return. Be sure he holds the down on your return until you say "Okay." At that point, he gets his treat—just so he'll remember for next time that it's not over until it's over.

THE COME EXERCISE

No command is more important to the safety of your Bull Terrier than "Come." It is what you should say every single time you see the puppy running toward you: "Binky, come! Good dog." During playtime, run a few feet away from the puppy and turn and tell him to "Come" as he is already running to you. You can go so far as to teach your puppy two things at once if you squat down and hold out your arms. As the pup gets close to you and you're saying "Good dog," bring your right arm in about waist high. Now he's also learning the hand signal, an excellent device should you be on the phone when you need to get him to come to you! You'll also both be one step ahead when you enter obedience classes.

"SCHOOL" MODE

When is your puppy ready for a lesson? Maybe not always when you are. Attempting training with treats just before his mealtime is asking for disaster. Notice which times of day he performs best and make that Fido's school time.

When the puppy responds to your well-timed "Come," try it with the puppy on the training leash. This time, catch him off guard, while he's sniffing a leaf or watching a bird: "Binky, come!" You may have to pause for a split second after his name to be sure you have his attention. If the puppy shows any sign of confusion, give the leash a mild jerk and take a couple of steps backward. Do not repeat the command. In this case, you should say "Good come" as he reaches you.

TIPS FOR TRAINING AND SAFETY

1. Whether on or off leash, practice only in a fenced area.
2. Remove the training collar when the training session is over.
3. Don't try to break up a dog-fight.
4. "Come," "Leave it" and "Wait" are safety commands.
5. The dog belongs in a crate or behind a barrier when riding in the car.
6. Don't ignore the dog's first sign of aggression. Aggression only gets worse, so take it seriously.
7. Keep the faces of children and dogs separated.
8. Pay attention to what the dog is chewing.
9. Keep the vet's number near your phone.
10. "Okay" is a useful release command.

That's the number-one rule of training. Each command word is given just once. Anything more is nagging. You'll also notice that all commands are one word only. Even when they are actually two words, you say them as one.

Never call the dog to come to you—with or without his name—if you are angry or intend to correct him for some misbehavior. When correcting the pup, you go to him. Your dog must always connect "come" with something pleasant and with your approval; then you can rely on his response.

Puppies, like children, have notoriously short attention spans, so don't overdo it with any of the training. Keep each lesson short. Break it up with a quick run around the yard or a ball toss, repeat the lesson and quit as soon as the pup gets it right. That way, you will always end with a "Good dog."

Although not a water dog by trade, many Bull Terriers enjoy aquatic activity.

A Bull Terrier is a very strong dog. You do not want him pulling *you* around. You must always be the one in control when your Bull Terrier's on the other end of the leash.

Life isn't perfect and neither are puppies. A time will come, often around 10 months of age, when he'll become "selectively deaf" or choose to "forget" his name. He may respond by wagging his tail (and even seeming to smile at you) with a look that says "Make me!" Laugh, throw his favorite toy and skip the lesson you had planned. Pups will be pups!

THE HEEL EXERCISE

The second most important command to teach, after the come, is the heel. When you are walking your growing puppy, you need to be in control. Besides, it looks terrible to be pulled and yanked down the street, and it's not much fun either. Your eight-to ten-week-old puppy will probably follow you everywhere, but that's his natural instinct, not your control over the situation. However, any time he does follow you, you can say "Heel" and be ahead of the game, as he will learn to associate this command with the action of following you before you even begin teaching him to heel.

There is a very precise, almost military, procedure for teaching your dog to heel. As with all other obedience training, begin with the dog on your left side. He will be in a very nice sit and you will have the training leash across your chest. Hold the loop and folded leash in your right hand. Pick up the slack leash above the dog in your left hand and hold it loosely

TEACHER'S PET

Dogs are individuals, not robots, with many traits basic to their breed. Some, bred to work alone, are independent thinkers; others rely on you to call the shots. If you have enrolled in a training class, your instructor can offer alternative methods of training based on your individual dog's instincts and personality. You may benefit from using a different type of collar or switching to a class with different kinds of dogs.

at your side. Step out on your left foot as you say "Heel." If the puppy does not move, give a gentle tug or pat your left leg to get him started. If he surges ahead of you, stop and pull him back gently until he is at your side. Tell him to sit and begin again.

Walk a few steps and stop while the puppy is correctly beside you. Tell him to sit and give mild verbal praise. (More enthusiastic praise will encourage him to think the lesson is over.) Repeat the lesson, increasing the number of steps you take only as long as the dog is heeling nicely beside you. When you end the lesson, have him hold the sit, then give him the "Okay" to let him know that this is the end of the lesson. Praise him so that he knows he did a good job.

The cure for excessive pulling (a common problem) is to stop when the dog is no more than 2 or 3 feet ahead of you. Guide him back into position and begin again. With a really determined puller, try switching to a head collar. This will automatically turn the pup's head toward you so you can bring him back easily to the heel position. Give quiet, reassuring praise every time the leash goes slack and he's staying with you.

Staying and heeling can take a lot out of a dog, so provide playtime and free-running exercise to shake off the stress when the lessons are over. You don't want him to associate training with all work and no fun.

TAPERING OFF TIDBITS

Your dog has been watching you—and the hand that treats— throughout all of his lessons, and now it's time to break the treat habit. Begin by giving him treats at the end of each lesson only. Then start to give a treat after the

LET'S GO!

Many people use "Let's go" instead of "Heel" when teaching their dogs to behave on lead. It sounds more like fun! When beginning to teach the heel, whatever command you use, always step off on your left foot. That's the one next to the dog, who is on your left side, in case you've forgotten. Keep a loose leash. When the dog pulls ahead, stop, bring him back and begin again. Use treats to guide him around turns.

TIME TO PLAY!

Playtime can happen both indoors and out. A young puppy is growing so rapidly that he needs sleep more than he needs a lot of physical exercise. Puppies get sufficient exercise on their own just through normal puppy activity. Monitor play with young children so you can remove the puppy when he's had enough, or calm the kids if they get too rowdy. Almost all puppies love to chase after a toy you've thrown, and you can turn your games into educational activities. Every time your puppy brings the toy back to you, say "Give it" (or "Drop it") followed by "Good dog" and throwing it again. If he's reluctant to give it to you, offer a small treat so that he drops the toy as he takes the treat. He will soon get the idea.

end of only some of the lessons. At the end of every lesson, as well as during the lessons, be consistent with the praise. Your pup now doesn't know whether he'll get a treat or not, but he should keep performing well just in case! Finally, you will stop giving treat rewards entirely. Save them for something brand-new that you want to teach him. Keep up the praise and you'll always have a "good dog."

OBEDIENCE CLASSES

The advantages of an obedience class are that your dog will have to learn amid the distractions of other people and dogs and that your mistakes will be quickly corrected by the trainer. Teaching your dog along with a qualified instructor and other handlers who may have more dog experience than you is another plus of the class environment. The instructor and other handlers can help you to find the most efficient way of teaching your dog a command or exercise. It's often easier to learn by other people's mistakes than your own. You will also learn all of the requirements for competitive obedience trials, in which you can earn titles and go on to advanced jumping and retrieving exercises, which are fun for many dogs. Obedience classes build the foundation needed for many other canine activities (in which we humans are allowed to participate, too!).

TRAINING FOR OTHER ACTIVITIES

Once your dog has basic obedience under his collar and is 12 months of age, you can enter the world of agility training. Dogs think agility is pure fun, like being turned loose in an amusement park full of obstacles! In addition to agility, there are competitive sports geared toward specific breeds or groups of breeds. Tracking, for example is open to all "nosey" dogs (which would include all dogs!). For

Bull Terriers are athletic, agile and eager to please. They respond positively to training for most activities, especially those that challenge body and mind.

those who like to volunteer, there is the wonderful feeling of owning a certified therapy dog and visiting hospices, nursing homes and veterans' homes to bring smiles, comfort and companionship to those who live there.

Around the house, your Bull Terrier can be taught to do some simple chores. You might teach him to carry a basket of household items or to fetch the morning newspaper. The kids can teach the dog all kinds of tricks, from playing hide-and-seek to balancing a biscuit on his nose. A family dog is what rounds out the family. Everything he does beyond sitting in your lap or gazing lovingly at you represents the bonus of owning a dog.

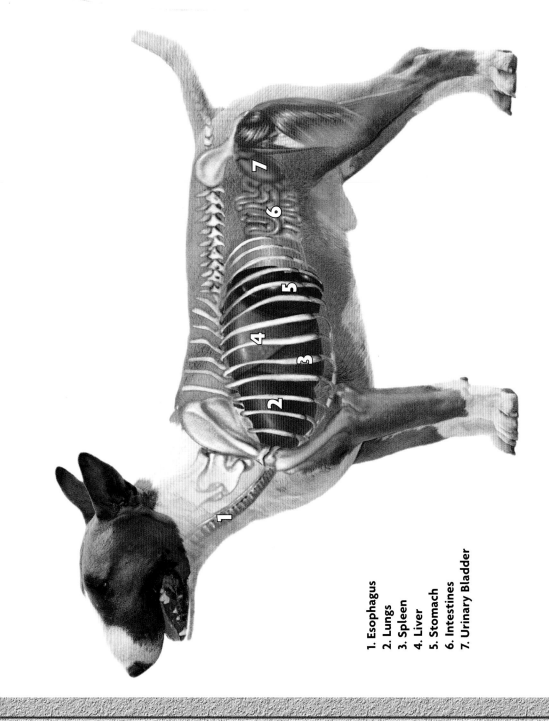

1. Esophagus
2. Lungs
3. Spleen
4. Liver
5. Stomach
6. Intestines
7. Urinary Bladder

INTERNAL ORGANS OF THE BULL TERRIER

HEALTHCARE OF YOUR

BULL TERRIER

By Lowell Ackerman DVM, DACVD

HEALTHCARE FOR A LIFETIME
When you own a dog, you become his healthcare advocate over his entire lifespan, as well as being the one to shoulder the financial burden of such care. Accordingly, it is worthwhile to focus on prevention rather than treatment, as you and your pet will both be happier.

Of course, the best place to have begun your program of preventive healthcare is with the initial purchase or adoption of your dog. There is no way of guaranteeing that your new friend is free of medical problems, but there are some things you can do to improve your odds. You certainly should have done adequate research into the Bull Terrier and have selected your puppy carefully rather than buying on impulse. Health issues aside, a large number of pet abandonment and relinquishment cases arise from a mismatch between pet needs and owner expectations. This is entirely preventable with appropriate planning and finding a good breeder.

Regarding healthcare issues specifically, it is very difficult to make blanket statements about where to acquire a problem-free pet, but, again, a reputable breeder is your best bet. In an ideal situation you have the opportunity to see both parents, get references from other owners of the breeder's pups and see genetic-testing documentation for several generations of the litter's ancestors. At the very least, you must thoroughly investigate the Bull Terrier and the problems inherent in that breed, as well as the genetic testing available to screen for those problems. Genetic testing offers some important benefits, but testing is available for only a few disorders in a relatively small number of breeds and is not available for some of the most common genetic diseases, such as hip dysplasia, cataracts, epilepsy,

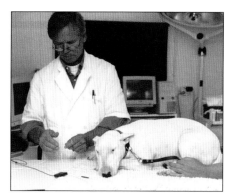

A qualified veterinarian is able to provide your Bull Terrier with all the care he requires, including recommendations for specialized testing and treatment.

DOGGIE DENTAL DON'TS

A veterinary dental exam is necessary if you notice one or any combination of the following in your dog:
- Broken, loose or missing teeth
- Loss of appetite (which could be due to mouth pain or illness caused by infection)
- Gum abnormalities, including redness, swelling and bleeding
- Drooling, with or without blood
- Yellowing of the teeth or gumline, indicating tartar
- Bad breath

cardiomyopathy, etc. This area of research is indeed exciting and increasingly important, and advances will continue to be made each year. In fact, recent research has shown that there is an equivalent dog gene for 75% of known human genes, so research done in either species is likely to benefit the other.

We've also discussed that evaluating the behavioral nature of your Bull Terrier and that of his immediate family members is an important part of the selection process that cannot be underestimated or overemphasized. It is sometimes difficult to evaluate temperament in puppies because certain behavioral tendencies, such as some forms of aggression, may not be immediately evident. More dogs are euthanized each year for behavioral reasons than for all medical conditions combined, so it is critical to take temperament issues seriously. Start with a well-balanced, friendly companion and put the time and effort into proper socialization, and you will both be rewarded with a lifelong valued relationship.

Assuming that you have started off with a pup from healthy, sound stock, you then become responsible for helping your veterinarian keep your pet healthy. Some crucial things happen before you even bring your puppy home. Parasite control typically begins at two weeks of age, and vaccinations typically begin at six to eight weeks of age. A pre-pubertal evaluation is typically scheduled for about six months of age. At this time, a dental evaluation is done (since the adult teeth are now in), heartworm prevention is started and neutering or spaying is most commonly done.

It is critical to commence regular dental care at home if you have not already done so. It may not sound very important, but most dogs have active periodontal disease by four years of age if they don't have their teeth cleaned regularly at home, not just at their veterinary exams. Dental problems lead to more than just bad "doggie breath." Gum disease can have very serious medical consequences. If you start brushing your dog's teeth and using antiseptic rinses from a young age, your dog will be accustomed to it and will not resist. The results will be healthy dentition, which your pet will need to enjoy a long, healthy life.

Most dogs are considered adults at a year of age, although some breeds still have some filling out to do up to about two or so years old. Even individual dogs within each breed have different healthcare requirements, so work with your veterinarian to determine what will be needed and what your role should be. This doctor-client relationship is important, because as vaccination guidelines change, there may not be an annual "vaccine visit" scheduled. You must make sure that you see your veterinarian at least annually, even if no vaccines are due, because this is the best opportunity to coordinate health-care activities and to make sure that no medical issues creep by unaddressed.

When your Bull Terrier reaches three-quarters of his anticipated lifespan, he is considered a "senior" and likely requires some special care. In general, if you've been taking great care of your canine companion throughout his formative and adult years, the transition to senior status should be a smooth one. Age is not a disease, and as long as everything is functioning as it should, there is no reason

YOUR DOG NEEDS TO VISIT THE VET IF:

• He has ingested a toxin such as antifreeze or a toxic plant; in these cases, administer first aid and call the vet right away
• His teeth are discolored, loose or missing or he has sores or other signs of infection or abnormality in the mouth
• He has been vomiting, has had diarrhea or has been constipated for over 24 hours; call immediately if you notice blood
• He has refused food for over 24 hours
• His eating habits, water intake or toilet habits have noticeably changed; if you have noticed weight gain or weight loss
• He shows symptoms of bloat, which requires *immediate* attention
• He is salivating excessively
• He has a lump in his throat
• He has a lump or bump anywhere on the body
• He is very lethargic
• He appears to be in pain or otherwise has trouble chewing or swallowing
• His skin loses elasticity

Of course, there will be other instances in which a visit to the vet is necessary; these are just some of the signs that could be indicative of serious problems that need to be caught as early as possible.

why most of late adulthood should not be rewarding for both you and your pet. This is especially true if you have tended to the details, such as regular veterinary visits, proper dental care, excellent nutrition and management of bone and joint issues.

At this stage in your Bull Terrier's life, your veterinarian will likely want to schedule visits twice yearly, instead of once, to run some laboratory screenings,

electrocardiograms and the like, and to change the diet to something more digestible. Catching problems early is the best way to manage them effectively. Treating the early stages of heart disease is so much easier than trying to intervene when there is more significant damage to the heart muscle. Similarly, managing the beginning of kidney problems is fairly routine if there is no significant kidney damage. Other problems, like cognitive dysfunction (similar to senility and Alzheimer's disease), cancer, diabetes and arthritis, are more common in older dogs, but all can be treated to help the dog live as many happy, comfortable years as possible. Just as in people, medical management is more effective (and less expensive) when you catch things early.

SELECTING A VETERINARIAN

There is probably no more important decision that you will make regarding your pet's health-care than the selection of his doctor. Your pet's veterinarian will be a pediatrician, family-practice physician and gerontologist, depending on the dog's life stage, and will be the individual who makes recommendations regarding issues such as when specialists need to be consulted, when diagnostic testing and/or therapeutic intervention is needed and when you will need to seek

TAKING YOUR DOG'S TEMPERATURE

It is important to know how to take your dog's temperature at times when you think he may be ill. It's not the most enjoyable task, but it can be done without too much difficulty. It's easier with a helper, preferably someone with whom the dog is friendly, so that one of you can hold the dog while the other inserts the thermometer.

Before inserting the thermometer, coat the end with petroleum jelly. Insert the thermometer slowly and gently into the dog's rectum about one inch. Wait for the reading, about two minutes. Be sure to remove the thermometer carefully and clean it thoroughly after each use.

A dog's normal body temperature is between 100.5 and 102.5 degrees F. Immediate veterinary attention is required if the dog's temperature is below 99 or above 104 degrees F.

outside emergency and critical-care services. Your vet will act as your advocate and liaison throughout these processes.

Everyone has his own idea about what to look for in a vet, an individual who will play a big role in his dog's (and, of course, his own) life for many years to come. For some, it is the compassionate caregiver with whom they hope to develop a professional relation-ship to span the lives of their dogs and even their future pets. For others, they are seeking a clinician with keen diagnostic and therapeutic insight who can deliver state-of-the-art healthcare. Still others need a veterinary facility that is open evenings and weekends, or is in close proximity or provides mobile veterinary services, to accommodate their schedules; these people may not much mind that their dogs might see different veterinarians on each visit. Just as we have different reasons for selecting our own healthcare professionals (e.g., covered by insurance plan, expert in field, convenient location, etc.), we should not expect that there is a one-size-fits-all recommendation for selecting a veterinarian and veterinary practice. The best advice is to be honest in your assessment of what you expect from a veterinary practice and to conscientiously research the options in your area. You will quickly appreciate that not all veterinary practices are the same, and you will be happiest with one that truly meets your needs.

There is another point to be considered in the selection of veterinary services. Not that long ago, a single veterinarian would attempt to manage all medical and surgical issues as they arose. That was often problematic, because veterinarians are trained in many species and many diseases, and it was just impossible for general veterinary practitioners to be experts in every species, every field and every ailment. However, just as in the human healthcare

INSURANCE

Pet insurance policies are very cost-effective (and very inexpensive by human health-insurance standards), but make sure that you buy the policy long before you intend to use it (preferably starting in puppyhood, because coverage will exclude pre-existing conditions) and that you are actually buying an indemnity insurance plan from an insurance company that is regulated by your state or province. Many insurance policy look-alikes are actually discount clubs that are redeemable only at specific locations and for specific services. An indemnity plan covers your pet at almost all veteri-nary, specialty and emergency practices and is an excellent way to manage your pet's ongoing healthcare needs.

fields, specialization has allowed general practitioners to concentrate on primary healthcare delivery, especially wellness and the prevention of infectious diseases, and to utilize a network of specialists to assist in the management of conditions that require specific expertise and experience. Thus there are now many types of veterinary specialists, including dermatologists, cardiologists, ophthalmologists, surgeons, internists, oncologists, neurologists, behaviorists, criticalists and others to help primary-care veterinarians deal with complicated medical challenges. In most cases, specialists see cases referred by primary-care veterinarians, make diagnoses and set up management plans. From there, the animals' ongoing care is returned to their primary-care veterinarians. This important team approach to your pet's medical-care needs has provided opportunities for advanced care and an unparalleled level of quality to be delivered.

With all of the opportunities for your Bull Terrier to receive high-quality veterinary medical care, there is another topic that needs to be addressed at the same time—cost. It's been said that you can have excellent healthcare or inexpensive healthcare, but never both; this is as true in veterinary medicine as it is in human medicine. While veterinary costs are a fraction of what the same services cost in the human healthcare arena, it is still difficult to deal with unanticipated medical costs, especially since they can easily creep into hundreds or even thousands of dollars if specialists or emergency services become involved. However, there are ways of managing these risks. The easiest is to buy pet health insurance and realize that its foremost purpose is not to cover routine healthcare visits but rather to serve as an umbrella for those rainy days when your pet needs medical care and you don't want to worry about whether or not you can afford that care.

VACCINATIONS AND INFECTIOUS DISEASES

There has never been an easier time to prevent a variety of infectious diseases in your dog, but the advances we've made in veterinary medicine come with a price—choice. Now while it may seem that choice is a good thing (and often it is), it has never been more difficult for the pet owner (or the veterinarian) to make an informed decision about the best way to protect pets through vaccination.

Years ago, it was just accepted that puppies got a starter series of vaccinations and then annual "boosters" throughout their lives to keep them protected. As more and more vaccines became

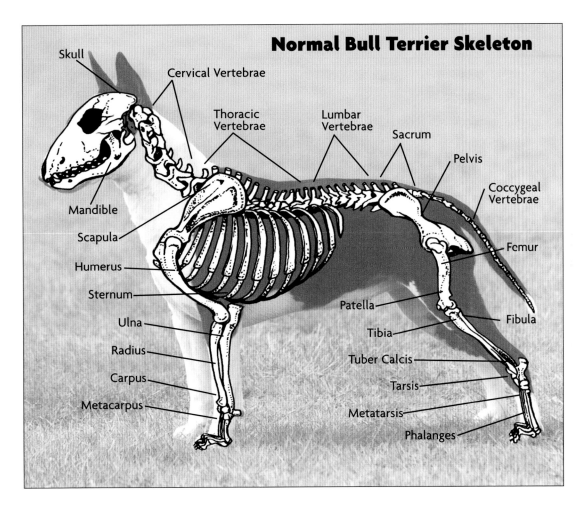

Normal Bull Terrier Skeleton

Skull
Cervical Vertebrae
Thoracic Vertebrae
Lumbar Vertebrae
Sacrum
Pelvis
Coccygeal Vertebrae
Mandible
Scapula
Humerus
Sternum
Ulna
Radius
Carpus
Metacarpus
Femur
Patella
Fibula
Tibia
Tuber Calcis
Tarsis
Metatarsis
Phalanges

available, consumers wanted the convenience of having all of that protection in a single injection. The result was "multivalent" vaccines that crammed a lot of protection into a single syringe. The manufacturers' recommendations were to give the vaccines annually, and this was a simple enough protocol to follow.

However, as veterinary medicine has become more sophisticated and we have started looking more at healthcare quandaries rather than convenience, it became necessary to reevaluate the situation and deal with some tough questions. It is important to realize that whether or not to use a particular vaccine depends on the risk of contracting the disease against which it protects, the severity of the disease if it is contracted, the duration of immunity provided by the vaccine, the safety of the product and the needs of the individual animal. In a very general sense, rabies, distemper, hepatitis and parvovirus are considered core vaccine needs, while parainfluenza, *Bordetella bronchiseptica*, leptospirosis, coronavirus and borreliosis (Lyme disease) are considered non-core needs and best reserved for animals that demonstrate reasonable risk of contracting the diseases.

NEUTERING/SPAYING

Sterilization procedures (neutering for males/spaying for females) are meant to accomplish several purposes. While the underlying premise is to address the risk of pet overpopulation, there are also some medical and behavioral benefits to the surgeries as well. For females, spaying prior to the first estrus (heat cycle) leads to a marked reduction in the risk of mammary cancer. There also will be no manifestations of "heat" to attract male dogs and no bleeding in the house. For males, there is prevention of testicular cancer and a reduction in the risk of prostate problems. In both sexes, there may be some limited reduction in aggressive behaviors toward other dogs and some diminishing of urine marking, roaming and mounting.

While neutering and spaying do indeed prevent animals from contributing to pet overpopulation, even no-cost and low-cost neutering options have not eliminated the problem. Perhaps one of the main reasons for this is that individuals who intentionally breed their dogs and those who allow their animals to run at large are the main causes of unwanted offspring. Also, animals in shelters are often there because they were abandoned or relinquished, not because they came from unplanned matings. Neutering/spaying is important, but it should be considered in the context of the real causes of animals' ending up in shelters and eventually being euthanized.

One of the important considerations regarding neutering is that it is a surgical procedure. This sometimes gets lost in discussions of low-cost procedures and commoditization of the process. In females, spaying is specifically referred to as an ovariohysterectomy. In this procedure, a midline incision is made in the abdomen and the entire uterus and both ovaries are surgically removed. While this is a major invasive surgical procedure, it usually has few complications, because it is typically performed on healthy young animals. However, it is major surgery, as any woman who

A curious Bull Terrier's explorations in the tall grass may bring home unwanted passengers in the form of fleas, ticks or other pests.

has had a hysterectomy will attest.

In males, neutering has traditionally referred to castration, which involves the surgical removal of both testicles. While still a significant piece of surgery, there is not the abdominal exposure that is required in the female surgery. In addition, there is now a chemical sterilization option, in which a solution is injected into each testicle, leading to atrophy of the sperm-producing cells. This can typically be done under sedation rather than full anesthesia. This is a relatively new approach, and there are no long-term clinical studies yet available.

Neutering/spaying is typically done around six months of age at most veterinary hospitals, although techniques have been pioneered to perform the procedures in animals as young as eight weeks of age. In general, the surgeries on the very young animals are done for the specific reason of sterilizing them before they go to their new homes. This is done in some shelter hospitals for assurance that the animals will definitely not produce any pups. Otherwise, these organizations need to rely on owners to comply with their wishes to have the animals "altered" at a later date, something that does not always happen.

There are some exciting immunocontraceptive "vaccines" currently under development, and there may be a time when contra-ception in pets will not require surgical procedures. We anxiously await these developments.

BULLY-SPECIFIC HEALTH CONCERNS

No breed of dog is without inherent health problems, and the Bull Terrier is no exception. For the most part, however, the breed is fairly healthy, without too many debilitating problems and genetic diseases. Most breeds of pure-bred dog can suffer from congenital or hereditary diseases that are passed on from the parents to the puppies. Bull Terriers do have some health problems unique to the breed, as well as some that affect many breeds of dog, but overall the Bully is hardy and is relatively free of genetic problems. Deafness is one problem that does occur and is seen more frequently in White Bull Terriers than Colored. Puppies should be tested, as otherwise it is difficult to determine if a youngster is deaf. The testing protocol, which Bully breeders should consider mandatory, is explained later in more detail. Another problem seen in Bull Terriers is a tendency to develop skin disorders, specifically allergies. All dogs have reactions to bites from insects, fleas and mosquitoes, but Bull Terriers tend to have more severe reactions than most other dogs. There are not many areas in which these pests do not exist, so it's important to try to limit your Bully's exposure to them and to use preventive treatments as recommended by your veterinarian.

Growing puppies sometimes experience lameness, which can occur suddenly and can be quite severe. This is a muscular breed whose frame is subject to much stress during the developmental period due to the dog's high activity level and rapid growth. A Bull Terrier pup that runs, jumps and plays hard is putting a lot of strain on his growing body. The joints are still fragile and cannot handle high-impact activity. This is why it is very important to monitor a pup's exercise and keep him from too-vigorous activity until he is mature.

As a dog ages, he becomes more susceptible to illness. A healthy Bull Terrier usually stays active well into his senior years, up to around 9 years of age. The average lifespan for the breed is around 12 years, but it's not uncommon for Bull Terriers to reach age 15 or older.

Bull Terriers are subject to many of the same ailments and health problems as are many other breeds of dog. However, there are a few health problems that seem to occur more frequently in Bull Terriers or are almost unique to Bull Terriers.

GI PROBLEMS

That's gastrointestinal and it involves the Bull Terrier's desire to swallow everything in his path. Owners find it difficult to diagnose this problem right away because most Bull Terriers don't show signs of discomfort or blockage for days. If your Bully is not acting like himself, is vomiting or is generally lethargic, there's a good chance he's eaten something exceptionally inedible. Count your shoes and call the vet for immediate assistance.

RENAL DISEASE

Unfortunately kidney problems in the Bull Terrier are fairly common and have been documented for many years. Many Bull Terriers are diagnosed as young puppies. In some lines, the kidneys are very small and undeveloped. In others, glomerular nephritis (malfunction of tiny filters in the kidney) causes kidney failure before age three. Sometimes affected dogs make it to age six to eight before dying from renal failure. It is recommended that a simple urine test called the urine protein/ urine creatinine (UP/UC) ratio be done annually—especially if you plan to breed your Bull Terrier— beginning at about 18 months to 2 years of age. Breeders are asked not to breed animals with an abnormal UP/UC ratio. Abnormal ratios indicate too much protein in the urine and should be evaluated further to determine the exact cause. Such dogs are more likely to develop kidney disease themselves or to produce puppies with kidney problems.

NEUROLOGICAL/BEHAVIORAL PECULIARITIES

Compulsive behaviors are not terribly uncommon in dogs, and Bull Terriers, depending on the individual's predisposition to compulsive behaviors and stress, can develop a few. Some Bull Terriers chase their tails, which may lead to more serious compulsions. In the mild form, tail chasing seems to be related to boredom or to stress of some kind. Some dogs merely spin around in circles a few times when they are excited. Usually, this is not a serious problem and can be remedied by removing the cause of the stress or boredom.

SPINNING

A much more serious form of tail chasing is called spinning or whirling. This compulsive behavior usually begins at about six months of age. Though it starts out as a "cute" form of entertainment for both dog and owner, some Bull Terriers become obsessed by their tails and may circle for hours. They lose interest in food and water. All attempts to get the dog to stop this behavior fail.

Fortunately, only a few Bull Terriers develop behavioral abnormalities. Most are normal, happy and playful like this roly-poly puppy.

Sometimes the dog yelps while spinning and may even attempt to bite his interfering owner.

Spinning is a most frustrating problem for owners to overcome, and euthanasia, unfortunately, has sometimes been the last resort. Studies have indicated that even amputating the dog's tail has not stopped the behavior. Veterinarians believe that there may be a connection between spinning and epilepsy or another seizure disorder. Most spinning dogs respond to treatment with phenobarbital either alone or in conjunction with other medications. Some of the less severe cases do well on anti-obsessive drugs such as Anafranil or Prozac. It is interesting that treatment of spinning Bull Terriers has been more successful in females than males. Be aware also that a disease may be expressed through compulsive behaviors, and you should discuss this possibility with your vet. Compulsive behaviors are likely hereditary, so discuss the possibility with your chosen breeder before you adopt your Bull Terrier.

RAGE SYNDROME

Yes, the Bull Terrier was originally bred for fighting, and the breed certainly can be aggressive, but generally the Bull Terrier should be friendly and peaceful most of the time. Incidents of unexplained aggres-

> **ADDITIONAL PROBLEMS**
> Patellar luxation (kneecap problems) and thyroid problems are seen in many breeds of dog, including the Bull Terrier. Bull Terriers should be tested for both of these hereditary disorders before breeding. For more information on these and the other health problems affecting the breed, owners are advised to check out the BTCA's website at www.btca.com.

sion toward human members of his own family by a dog that usually behaves normally may signify rage. A Bull Terrier with rage is an extremely frightening and dangerous dog. The episodes are usually unpredictable. Some owners claim that the dog gets a glazed look in his eyes before a "spell." Rage is presently considered to be another seizure-type disorder. Some of the severe spinners develop rage-like symptoms as the spinning becomes worse. Prognosis is poor.

It is important not to confuse dominant aggression with rage. Rage syndrome is neurological in nature and is not caused by environmental factors. Aggressive tendencies can be linked to the dog's environment, relationships and experience; training and proper handling can solve aggression problems whereas they cannot help dogs that suffer from rage.

EPILEPSY

Epilepsy in Bull Terriers can be inherited, manifested as grand-mal-type epileptic seizures. Affected dogs experience seizures when they are 6 to 18 months of age, though the episodes can begin later depending on the dog. Owners have had good success controlling seizures through medication even though the long-term prognosis is guarded. The life expectancy of affected dogs can be as short as one year after the beginning of the seizures. The drug commonly used to ward off seizures is known as phenobarbital; unfortunately extended use of the drug can result in liver failure.

HEART DISEASE

Hereditary heart problems affect many breeds of pure-bred dogs and the Bull Terrier is not excluded. There are various kinds of heart murmurs caused by different structural problems in the heart. Some are more serious than others. A vet will listen to the dog's heart to try to detect a heart murmur and determine its severity. If a heart murmur is detected in a puppy, he may outgrow it if it is very minor. However, if the murmur is more serious or if a minor murmur becomes worse, the vet may recommend further diagnostic tests such as cardiac ultrasound. Defects in heart structure and function are potentially life-threatening, although some Bull Terriers live with their heart murmurs for many years. Needless to say, dogs with heart defects should not be bred.

DEAFNESS

Since hereditary deafness has long been documented in Bull Terriers, both Whites and Coloreds, this is a major concern of breeders and potential owners. Most breed

Health and behavioral concerns are far more important than the cosmetic requirements of conformation. This handsome, healthy Bully would be disqualified from showing for the patch over his tail, but that's no problem for the pet owner who wants a sound companion animal more than a show specimen.

historians link the disorder to the Dalmatian blood flowing in the breed's ancestors, though others point back even further to the English White Terrier.

All Bull Terrier puppies should be tested for deafness by the BAER (Brainstem Auditory Evoked Response) test. A simple explanation of this text is that it is a painless procedure in which sounds are administered to the dog, and then the sound waves are analyzed to see if they are picked up by the dog's ears and transmitted to the brain. Small electrodes inserted under the dog's skin analyze the sound waves transmission from the ear drum to the cochlea and eventually to the brain. Your veterinarian, your breeder or a Bull Terrier club should be able to help you find the nearest BAER testing facility (usually at veterinary schools or clinics held by your regional club). Each ear is tested separately. Most Bull Terriers have normal hearing in both ears. Some Whites are deaf in both ears (bilaterally deaf) while some Whites and Coloreds are deaf in one ear (unilaterally deaf).

Strangely enough, even animals with normal hearing can produce puppies who are deaf in one ear if there are deaf Bull Terriers among their ancestors. Bull Terriers who are deaf in one ear seem to lead fairly normal lives. The most obvious difference from a normal dog is their difficulty in determining the direction of sound. A unilaterally deaf pup may seem bewildered as he tries to figure out where a sound comes from. No doubt such puppies have been in the breed for many years. The BAER test makes their identification possible and it is recommended that the test be performed on young puppies, although adults can be tested, too. This is a standard test and should be considered if you think that your Bull Terrier may suffer from deafness. It is an absolutely necessary test for Bull Terriers with breeding potential.

SKIN PROBLEMS IN BULL TERRIERS
Veterinarians are consulted by dog owners for skin problems more than any other group of

To help manage the deafness problems in the breed, BAER testing is performed at special facilities around the world.

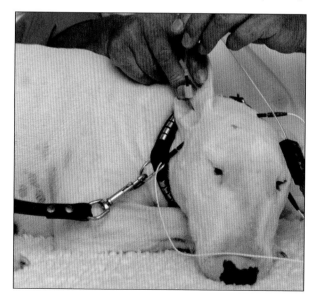

diseases or maladies. Dogs' skin is almost as sensitive as human skin and both suffer almost the same ailments, including acne in the Bull Terrier. For this reason, veterinary dermatology has developed into a specialty practiced by many vets.

Some Bull Terriers, particularly White Bull Terriers, may suffer from severe skin problems. Possibly there is a connection between faults with the immune system and this severe dermatitis. Some dogs respond well to dietary changes to more natural-type foods with few or no chemical additives. Others may require long-term treatment with antibiotics and/or steroids. Seek the advice of a veterinarian if your Bull Terrier seems to have frequent skin problems.

Since many skin problems have visual symptoms that are almost identical, it requires the skill of an experienced veterinary dermatologist to identify and cure many of the more severe skin disorders. Pet shops sell many treatments for skin problems, but most of the treatments are directed at symptoms and not the underlying problem(s). If your dog is suffering from a skin disorder, you should seek professional assistance as quickly as possible. As with all diseases, the earlier a problem is identified and treated, the more likely it is that the cure will be successful.

Many skin disorders are inherited and some are fatal. For example, acrodermatitis is an inherited disease that is transmitted by both parents. The parents, who appear (phenotypically) normal, have a recessive gene for acrodermatitis, meaning that they carry, but are not affected by, the disease.

This is an immune problem associated with zinc deficiency, and appears to be peculiar to the Bull Terrier breed. The disorder is recognizable in young puppies, some of whom may die shortly after birth because they are too lethargic to nurse. Others do fairly well until weaning. When they are no longer receiving antibodies from their mothers,

COMMON INFECTIOUS DISEASES IN CANINES

Let's discuss some of the diseases that create the need for vaccinating dogs in the first place. Following are the major canine infectious diseases and a simple explanation of each.

Rabies: A devastating viral disease that can be fatal in dogs and people. In fact, vaccination of dogs and cats is an important public-health measure to create a resistant animal buffer population to protect people from contracting the disease. Vaccination schedules are determined on a government level and are not optional for pet owners; rabies vaccination is required by law in all 50 states.

Parvovirus: A severe, potentially life-threatening disease that is easily transmitted between dogs. There are four strains of the virus, but it is believed that there is significant "cross-protection" between strains that may be included in individual vaccines.

Distemper: A potentially severe and life-threatening disease with a relatively high risk of exposure, especially in certain regions. In very high-risk distemper environments, young pups may be vaccinated with human measles vaccine, a related virus that offers cross-protection when administered at four to ten weeks of age.

Hepatitis: Caused by canine adenovirus type 1 (CAV-1), but since vaccination with the causative virus has a higher rate of adverse effects, cross-protection is derived from the use of adenovirus type 2 (CAV-2), a cause of respiratory disease and one of the potential causes of canine cough. Vaccination with CAV-2 provides long-term immunity against hepatitis, but relatively less protection against respiratory infection.

Canine cough: Also called tracheobronchitis, actually a fairly complicated result of viral and bacterial offenders; therefore, even with vaccination, protection is incomplete. Wherever dogs congregate, canine cough will likely be spread among them. Intranasal vaccination with *Bordetella* and parainfluenza is the best safeguard, but the duration of immunity does not appear to be very long, typically a year at most. These are non-core vaccines, but vaccination is sometimes mandated by boarding kennels, obedience classes, dog shows and other places where dogs congregate to try to minimize spread of infection.

Leptospirosis: A potentially fatal disease that is more common in some geographic regions. It is capable of being spread to humans. The disease varies with the individual "serovar," or strain, of *Leptospira* involved. Since there does not appear to be much cross-protection between serovars, protection is only as good as the likelihood that the serovar in the vaccine is the same as the one in the pet's local environment. Problems with *Leptospira* vaccines are that protection does not last very long, side effects are not uncommon and a large percentage of dogs (perhaps 30%) may not respond to vaccination.

Borrelia burgdorferi: The cause of Lyme disease, the risk of which varies with the geographic area in which the pet lives and travels. Lyme disease is spread by deer ticks in the eastern US and western black-legged ticks in the western part of the country, and the risk of exposure is high in some regions. Lameness, fever and inappetence are most commonly seen in affected dogs. The extent of protection from the vaccine has not been conclusively demonstrated.

Coronavirus: This disease has a high risk of exposure, especially in areas where dogs congregate, but it typically causes only mild to moderate digestive upset (diarrhea, vomiting, etc.). Vaccines are available, but the duration of protection is believed to be relatively short and the effectiveness of the vaccine in preventing infection is considered low.

There are many other vaccinations available, including those for *Giardia* and canine adenovirus-1. While there may be some specific indications for their use, and local risk factors to be considered, they are not widely recommended for most dogs.

HIT ME WITH A HOT SPOT

What is a hot spot? Technically known as pyotraumatic dermatitis, a hot spot is an infection on the dog's coat, usually by the rear end, under the tail or on a leg, which the dog inflicts upon himself. The dog licks and bites the itchy spot until it becomes inflamed and infected. The hot spot can range in size from the circumference of a grape to the circumference of an apple. Provided that the hot spot is not related to a deeper bacterial infection, it can be treated topically by clipping the area, cleaning the sore and giving prednisone. For bacterial infections, antibiotics are required. In some cases, an Elizabethan collar is required to keep the dog from further irritating the hot spot. The itching can intensify and the pain becomes worse. Medicated shampoos and cool compresses, drying agents and topical steroids may be prescribed by your vet as well.

Hot spots can be caused by fleas, an allergy, an ear infection, anal sac problems, mange or a foreign irritant. Likewise, they can be linked to psychoses. The underlying problem must be addressed in addition to the hot spot itself.

mouth is domed and has deeper than normal ridges. The food gets stuck, so puppies have to be hand fed a finely ground gruel-type food. Their growth rate slows so that they become runty-looking compared to their litter-mates. In some pups, there may be what seem to be neurological peculiarities such as abnormal gait (hindquarters particularly) or inability to wag the tail. Nasty rage-like temperaments may be seen in these puppies. Changes in coat color occur, with black coat or black patches tending to turn brownish. If not put down, these puppies usually succumb to infection.

Acrodermatitis is just one example of how difficult it is to prevent congenital dog diseases. The cost and skills required to ascertain whether two dogs should be mated are too high, even though Bull Terriers with acrodermatitis rarely reach breeding age and therefore screen themselves out of a program.

Other inherited skin problems are usually not as fatal as acrodermatitis. All skin diseases, inherited or otherwise, must be diagnosed and treated by a veterinary specialist. There are active programs being undertaken by many veterinary pharmaceutical manufacturers to solve most, if not all, of the common skin problems of dogs.

they tend to develop skin lesions, particularly between the toes and on the muzzle. Some also have difficulty eating solid foods because the roof of the

S. E. M. BY DR. DENNIS KUNKEL, UNIVERSITY OF HAWAII

A scanning electron micrograph of a dog flea, Ctenocephalides canis, on dog hair.

EXTERNAL PARASITES

FLEAS

Fleas have been around for millions of years and, while we have better tools now for controlling them than at any time in the past, there still is little chance that they will end up on an endangered species list. Actually, they are very well adapted to living on our pets, and they continue to adapt as we make advances.

The female flea can consume 15 times her weight in blood during active reproduction and can lay as many as 40 eggs a day. These eggs are very resistant to the effects of insecticides. They hatch into larvae, which then mature and spin cocoons. The immature fleas reside in this pupal stage until the time is right for feeding. This pupal stage is also very resistant to the effects of insecticides, and pupae can last in the environment without feeding for many months. Newly emergent fleas are attracted to animals by the warmth of the animals' bodies, movement and exhaled carbon dioxide. However, when they first emerge from their cocoons, they orient towards light; thus when an animal passes between a flea and the light source, casting a shadow, the flea pounces and starts to feed. If the animal turns out to be a dog or cat, the reproductive cycle continues. If the flea lands on another type of animal, including a person, the flea will bite but will then look for a more appropriate host. An emerging adult flea can survive without feeding for up to 12 months but, once it tastes blood, it can survive off its host for only three to four days.

It was once thought that fleas spend most of their lives in the environment, but we now know that fleas won't willingly jump off a dog unless leaping to another dog or when physically removed by brushing, bathing or other manipulation. Flea eggs, on the other hand, are shiny and smooth, and they roll off the animal and into the environment. The eggs, larvae and pupae then exist in the environment, but once the adult finds a susceptible animal, it's home sweet home until the flea is forced to seek refuge elsewhere.

Since adult fleas live on the animal and immature forms survive in the environment, a successful treatment plan must address all stages of the flea life cycle. There are now several safe and effective flea-control products

FLEA PREVENTION FOR YOUR DOG

- Discuss with your veterinarian the safest product to protect your dog, likely in the form of a monthly tablet or a liquid preparation placed on the back of the dog's neck.
- For dogs suffering from flea-bite dermatitis, a shampoo or topical insecticide treatment is required.
- Your lawn and property should be sprayed with an insecticide designed to kill fleas and ticks that lurk outdoors.
- Using a flea comb, check the dog's coat regularly for any signs of parasites.
- Practice good housekeeping. Vacuum floors, carpets and furniture regularly, especially in the areas that the dog frequents, and wash the dog's bedding weekly.
- Follow up house-cleaning with carpet shampoos and sprays to rid the house of fleas at all stages of development. Insect growth regulators are the safest option.

that can be applied on a monthly basis. These include fipronil, imidacloprid, selamectin and permethrin (found in several formulations). Most of these products have significant flea-killing rates within 24 hours. However, none of them will control the immature forms in the environment. To accomplish this, there are a variety of insect growth regulators that can be sprayed into

THE FLEA'S LIFE CYCLE

What came first, the flea or the egg? This age-old mystery is more difficult to comprehend than the actual cycle of the flea. Fleas usually live only about four months. A female can lay 2,000 eggs in her lifetime.

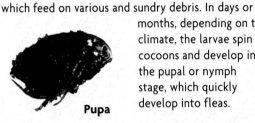

Egg

After ten days of rolling around your carpet or under your furniture, the eggs hatch into larvae, which feed on various and sundry debris. In days or months, depending on the climate, the larvae spin cocoons and develop into the pupal or nymph stage, which quickly develop into fleas.

Larva

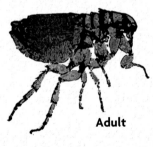

Pupa

These immature fleas must locate a host within 10 to 14 days or they will die. Only about 1% of the flea population exist as adult fleas, while the other 99% exist as eggs, larvae or pupae.

Adult

Photo by Carolina Biological Supply Co.

KILL FLEAS THE NATURAL WAY

If you choose not to go the route of conventional medication, there are some natural ways to ward off fleas:

- Dust your dog with a natural flea powder, composed of such herbal goodies as rosemary, wormwood, pennyroyal, citronella, rue, tobacco powder and eucalyptus.
- Apply diatomaceous earth, the fossilized remains of single-cell algae, to your carpets, furniture and pet's bedding. Even though it's not good for dogs, it's even worse for fleas, which will dry up swiftly and die.
- Brush your dog frequently, give him adequate exercise and let him fast occasionally. All of these activities strengthen the dog's system and make him more resistant to disease and parasites.
- Bathe your dog with a capful of pennyroyal or eucalyptus oil.
- Feed a natural diet, free of additives and preservatives. Add some fresh garlic and brewer's yeast to the dog's morning portion, as these items have flea-repelling properties.

the environment (e.g., pyriprox-yfen, methoprene, fenoxycarb) as well as insect development inhibitors such as lufenuron that can be administered. These compounds have no effect on adult fleas, but they stop immature forms from developing into adults. In years gone by we relied heavily on toxic insecti-cides (such as organophosphates, organochlorines and carbamates) to manage the flea problem, but today's options are not only much safer to use on our pets but also safer for the environment.

TICKS

Ticks are members of the spider class (arachnids) and are blood-sucking parasites capable of transmitting a variety of diseases, including Lyme disease, ehrlichiosis, babesiosis and Rocky Mountain spotted fever. It's easy to see ticks on your own skin, but it is more of a challenge when your dog is affected. Whenever you happen to be planning a stroll in a tick-infested area (especially forests, grassy or wooded areas or parks) be prepared to do a thorough inspection of your dog afterward to search for ticks. Ticks can be tricky, so make sure you spend time looking in the ears, between the toes and everywhere else where a tick might hide. Ticks need to be attached for 24–72 hours before they transmit most of the diseases that they carry, so you do have a window of opportunity for some preventive intervention.

Female ticks live to eat and

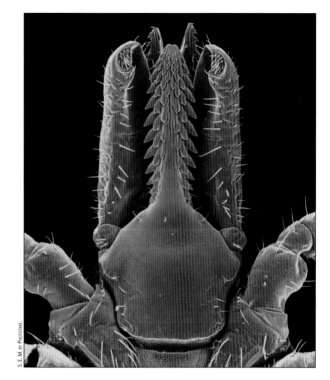

S. E. M. BY PHOTOTAKE.

breed. They can lay between 4,000 and 5,000 eggs and they die soon after. Males, on the other hand, live only to mate with the females and continue the process as long as they are able. Most ticks live on multiple hosts before parasitizing dogs. The immature forms typically reside on grass and shrubs, waiting for susceptible animals to walk by. The larvae and nymph stages typically feed on wildlife.

If only a few ticks are present on a dog, they can be plucked out, but it is important to remove the entire head and mouthparts, which may be deeply embedded

A scanning electron micrograph of the head of a female deer tick, *Ixodes dammini*, a parasitic tick that carries Lyme disease.

A TICKING BOMB

There is nothing good about a tick's harpooning his nose into your dog's skin. Among the diseases caused by ticks are Rocky Mountain spotted fever, canine ehrlichiosis, canine babesiosis, canine hepatozoonosis and Lyme disease. If a dog is allergic to the saliva of a female wood tick, he can develop tick paralysis.

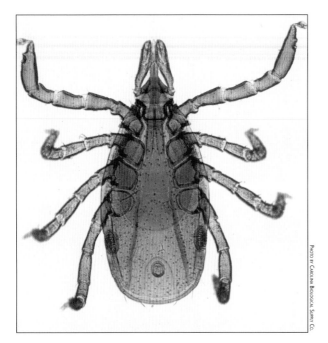

Deer tick,
Ixodes dammini.

disposed of in a container of alcohol or household bleach.

Some of the newer flea products, specifically those with fipronil, selamectin and permethrin, have effect against some, but not all, species of tick. Flea collars containing appropriate pesticides (e.g., propoxur, chlorfenvinphos) can aid in tick control. In most areas, such collars should be placed on animals in March, at the beginning of the tick season, and changed regularly. Leaving the collar on when the pesticide level is waning invites the development of resistance. Amitraz collars are also good for tick control, and the active ingredient does not interfere with other flea-control products. The ingredient helps prevent the attachment of ticks to the skin and will cause those ticks already on the skin to detach themselves.

in the skin. This is best accomplished with forceps designed especially for this purpose; fingers can be used but should be protected with rubber gloves, plastic wrap or at least a paper towel. The tick should be grasped as closely as possible to the animal's skin and should be pulled upward with steady, even pressure. Do not squeeze, crush or puncture the body of the tick or you risk exposure to any disease carried by that tick. Once the ticks have been removed, the sites of attachment should be disinfected. Your hands should then be washed with soap and water to further minimize risk of contagion. The tick should be

TICK CONTROL

Removal of underbrush and leaf litter and the thinning of trees in areas where tick control is desired are recommended. These actions remove the cover and food sources for small animals that serve as hosts for ticks. With continued mowing of grasses in these areas, the probability of ticks' surviving is further reduced. A variety of insecticide ingredients (e.g., resmethrin, carbaryl, permethrin, chlorpyrifos, dioxathion and allethrin) are registered for tick control around the home.

MITES

Mites are tiny arachnid parasites that parasitize the skin of dogs. Skin diseases caused by mites are referred to as "mange," and there are many different forms seen in dogs. These forms are very different from one another, each one warranting an individual description.

Sarcoptic mange, or scabies, is one of the itchiest conditions that affects dogs. The microscopic *Sarcoptes* mites burrow into the superficial layers of the skin and can drive dogs crazy with itchiness. They are also communicable to people, although they can't complete their reproductive cycle on people. In addition to being tiny, the mites also are often difficult to find when trying to make a diagnosis. Skin scrapings from multiple areas are examined microscopically but, even then, sometimes the mites cannot be found.

Fortunately, scabies is relatively easy to treat, and there are a variety of products that will successfully kill the mites. Since the mites can't live in the environment for very long without feeding, a complete cure is usually possible within four to eight weeks.

Cheyletiellosis is caused by a relatively large mite, which sometimes can be seen even without a microscope. Often referred to as "walking dandruff," this also causes itching, but not usually as profound as with scabies.

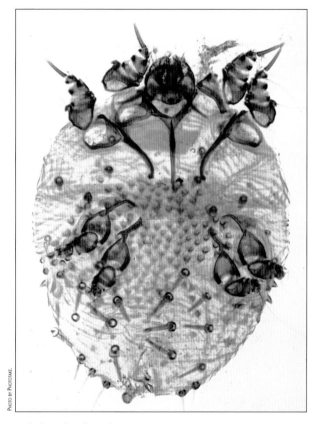

PHOTO BY PHOTOTAKE.

Sarcoptes scabiei, commonly known as the "itch mite."

While *Cheyletiella* mites can survive somewhat longer in the environment than scabies mites, they too are relatively easy to treat, being responsive to not only the medications used to treat scabies but also often to flea-control products.

Otodectes cynotis is the canine ear mite and is one of the more common causes of mange, especially in young dogs in shelters or pet stores. That's because the mites are typically present in large numbers and are quickly spread to

Micrograph of a dog louse, *Heterodoxus spiniger*. Female lice attach their eggs to the hairs of the dog. As the eggs hatch, the larval lice bite and feed on the blood. Lice can also feed on dead skin and hair. This feeding activity can cause hair loss and skin problems.

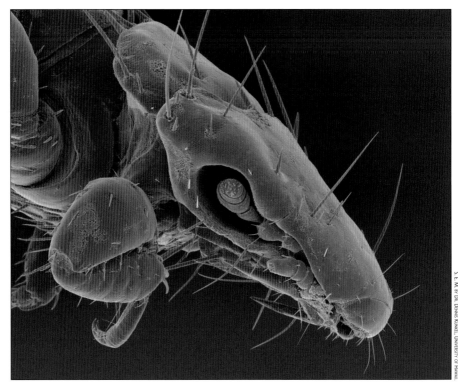

S. E. M. BY DR. DENNIS KUNKEL, UNIVERSITY OF HAWAII.

nearby animals. The mites rarely do much harm but can be difficult to eradicate if the treatment regimen is not comprehensive. While many try to treat the condition with ear drops only, this is the most common cause of treatment failure. Ear drops cause the mites to simply move out of the ears and as far away as possible (usually to the base of the tail) until the insecticide levels in the ears drop to an acceptable level—then it's back to business as usual! The successful treatment of ear mites requires treating all animals in the household with a systemic insecticide, such as selamectin, or a

combination of miticidal ear drops combined with whole-body flea-control preparations.

Demodicosis, sometimes referred to as red mange, can be one of the most difficult forms of mange to treat. Part of the problem has to do with the fact that the mites live in the hair follicles and they are relatively well shielded from topical and systemic products. The main issue, however, is that demodectic mange typically results only when there is some underlying process interfering with the dog's immune system.

Since *Demodex* mites are

normal residents of the skin of mammals, including humans, there is usually a mite population explosion only when the immune system fails to keep the number of mites in check. In young animals, the immune deficit may be transient or may reflect an actual inherited immune problem. In older animals, demodicosis is usually seen only when there is another disease hampering the immune system, such as diabetes, cancer, thyroid problems or the use of immune-suppressing drugs. Accordingly, treatment involves not only trying to kill the mange mites but also discerning what is interfering with immune function and correcting it if possible.

Chiggers represent several different species of mite that don't parasitize dogs specifically, but do latch on to passersby and can cause irritation. The problem is most prevalent in wooded areas in the late summer and fall. Treatment is not difficult, as the mites do not complete their life cycle on dogs and are susceptible to a variety of miticidal products.

MOSQUITOES

Mosquitoes have long been known to transmit a variety of diseases to people, as well as just being biting pests during warm weather. They also pose a real risk to pets. Not only do they carry deadly heartworms but recently there also has been much concern over their involvement with West Nile virus. While we can avoid heartworm with the use of preventive medications, there are no such preventives for West Nile virus. The only method of prevention in endemic areas is active mosquito control. Fortunately, most dogs that have been exposed to the virus only developed flu-like symptoms and, to date, there have not been the large number of reported deaths in canines as seen in some other species.

ILLUSTRATION BY PHOTOTAKE

Illustration of *Demodex folliculoram.*

MOSQUITO REPELLENT

Low concentrations of DEET (less than 10%), found in many human mosquito repellents, have been safely used in dogs but, in these concentrations, probably give only about two hours of protection. DEET may be safe in these small concentrations, but since it is not licensed for use on dogs, there is no research proving its safety for dogs. Products containing permethrin give the longest-lasting protection, perhaps two to four weeks. As DEET is not licensed for use on dogs, and both DEET and permethrin can be quite toxic to cats, appropriate care should be exercised. Other products, such as those containing oil of citronella, also have some mosquito-repellent activity, but typically have a relatively short duration of action.

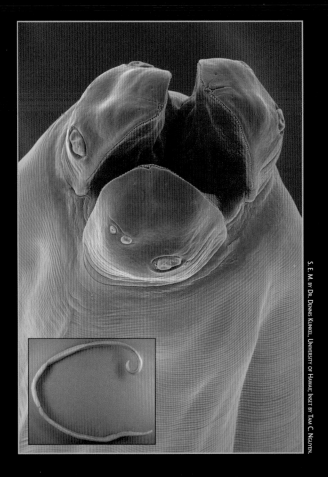

ASCARID DANGERS

The most commonly encountered worms in dogs are roundworms known as ascarids. *Toxascaris leonine* and *Toxocara canis* are the two species that infect dogs. Subsisting in the dog's stomach and intestines, adult roundworms can grow to 7 inches in length and adult females can lay in excess of 200,000 eggs in a single day.

In humans, visceral larval migrans affects people who have ingested eggs of *Toxocara canis*, which frequently contaminates children's sandboxes, beaches and park grounds. The roundworms reside in the human's stomach and intestines, as they would in a dog's, but do not mature. Instead, they find their way to the liver, lungs and skin, or even to the heart or kidneys in severe cases. Deworming puppies is critical in preventing the infection in humans, and young children should never handle nursing pups who have not been dewormed.

The ascarid roundworm *Toxocara canis*, showing the mouth with three lips. INSET: Photomicrograph of the roundworm *Ascaris lumbricoides.*

INTERNAL PARASITES: WORMS

ASCARIDS

Ascarids are intestinal roundworms that rarely cause severe disease in dogs. Nonetheless, they are of major public health significance because they can be transferred to people. Sadly, it is children who are most commonly affected by the parasite, probably from inadvertently ingesting ascarid-contaminated soil. In fact, many yards and children's sandboxes contain appreciable numbers of ascarid eggs. So, while ascarids don't bite dogs or latch onto their intestines to suck blood, they do cause some nasty medical conditions in children and are best eradicated from our furry friends. Because pups can start passing ascarid eggs by three weeks of age, most parasite-control programs begin at two weeks of age and are repeated every two weeks until pups are eight weeks old. It is important to

HOOKED ON ANCYLOSTOMA

Adult dogs can become infected by the bloodsucking nematodes we commonly call hookworms via ingesting larvae from the ground or via the larvae penetrating the dog's skin. It is not uncommon for infected dogs to show no symptoms of hookworm infestation. Sometimes symptoms occur within ten days of exposure. These symptoms can include bloody diarrhea, anemia, loss of weight and general weakness. Dogs pass the hookworm eggs in their stools, which serves as the vet's method of identifying the infestation. The hookworm larvae can encyst themselves in the dog's tissues and be released when the dog is experiencing stress.

Caused by an *Ancylostoma* species whose common host is the dog, cutaneous larval migrans affects humans, causing itching and lumps and streaks beneath the surface of the skin.

S. E. M. by Dr. Dennis Kunkel, University of Hawaii.

realize that bitches can pass ascarids to their pups even if they test negative prior to whelping. Accordingly, bitches are best treated at the same time as the pups.

HOOKWORMS

Unlike ascarids, hookworms do latch onto a dog's intestinal tract and can cause significant loss of blood and protein. Similar to ascarids, hookworms can be transmitted to humans, where they cause a condition known as cutaneous larval migrans. Dogs can become infected either by consuming the infective larvae or by the larvae's penetrating the skin directly. People most often get infected when they are lying on the ground (such as on a beach) and the larvae penetrate the skin. Yes, the larvae can penetrate through a beach blanket. Hookworms are typically susceptible to the same medications used to treat ascarids.

The hookworm *Ancylostoma caninum* infests the intestines of dogs. INSET: Note the row of hooks at the posterior end, used to anchor the worm to the intestinal wall.

WHIPWORMS

Whipworms latch onto the lower aspects of the dog's colon and can cause cramping and diarrhea. Eggs do not start to appear in the dog's feces until about three months after the dog was infected. This worm has a peculiar life cycle, which makes it more difficult to control than ascarids or hookworms. The good thing is that whipworms rarely are transferred to people.

Some of the medications used to treat ascarids and hookworms are also effective against whipworms, but, in general, a separate treatment protocol is needed. Since most of the medications are effective against the adults but not the eggs or larvae, treatment is typically repeated in three weeks, and then often in three

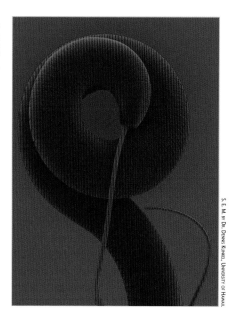

Adult whipworm, *Trichuris* sp., an intestinal parasite.

S. E. M. BY DR. DENNIS KUNKEL, UNIVERSITY OF HAWAII

> ### WORM-CONTROL GUIDELINES
> • Practice sanitary habits with your dog and home.
> • Clean up after your dog and don't let him sniff or eat other dogs' droppings.
> • Control insects and fleas in the dog's environment. Fleas, lice, cockroaches, beetles, mice and rats can act as hosts for various worms.
> • Prevent dogs from eating uncooked meat, raw poultry and dead animals.
> • Keep dogs and children from playing in sand and soil.
> • Kennel dogs on cement or gravel; avoid dirt runs.
> • Administer heartworm preventives regularly.
> • Have your vet examine your dog's stools at your annual visits.
> • Select a boarding kennel carefully so as to avoid contamination from other dogs or an unsanitary environment.
> • Prevent dogs from roaming. Obey local leash laws.

months as well. Unfortunately, since dogs don't develop resistance to whipworms, it is difficult to prevent them from getting reinfected if they visit soil contaminated with whipworm eggs.

TAPEWORMS

There are many different species of tapeworm that affect dogs, but *Dipylidium caninum* is probably the most common and is spread by fleas. Flea larvae feed on organic debris and tapeworm eggs in the environment and, when a dog chews at himself and manages to ingest fleas, he might get a dose of tapeworm at the same time. The tapeworm then develops further in the intestine of the dog.

The tapeworm itself, which is a parasitic flatworm that latches onto the intestinal wall, is composed of numerous segments. When the segments break off into the intestine (as proglottids), they may accumulate around the rectum, like grains of rice. While this tapeworm is disgusting in its behavior, it is not directly communicable to humans (although humans can also get infected by swallowing fleas).

A much more dangerous flatworm is *Echinococcus multilocularis*, which is typically found in foxes, coyotes and wolves. The eggs are passed in the feces and infect rodents, and, when dogs eat the rodents, the dogs can be infected by thousands of adult tapeworms. While the parasites don't cause many problems in dogs, this is considered the most lethal worm infection that people can get. Take appropriate precautions if you live in an area in which these tapeworms are found. Do not use mulch that may contain feces of dogs, cats or wildlife, and

discourage your pets from hunting wildlife. Treat these tapeworm infections aggressively in pets, because if humans get infected, approximately half die.

HEARTWORMS

Heartworm disease is caused by the parasite *Dirofilaria immitis* and is seen in dogs around the world. A member of the roundworm group, it is spread between dogs by the bite of an infected mosquito. The mosquito injects infective larvae into the dog's skin with its bite, and these larvae develop under the skin for a period of time before making their way to the heart. There they develop into adults, which grow and create blockages of the heart, lungs and major blood vessels there. They also start producing offspring (microfilariae) and these microfi-

A dog tapeworm proglottid (body segment).

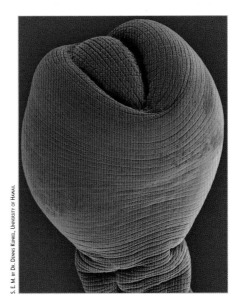

The dog tapeworm *Taenia pisiformis.*

S. E. M. BY DR. DENNIS KUNKEL, UNIVERSITY OF HAWAII.

A Look at Internal Parasites

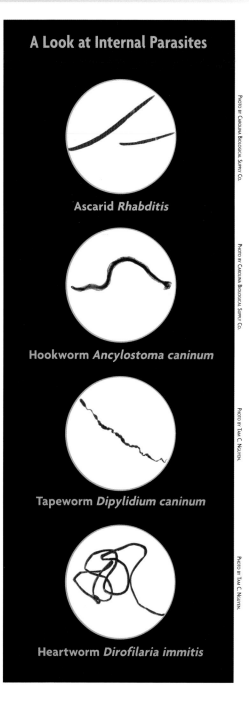

Ascarid *Rhabditis*

Hookworm *Ancylostoma caninum*

Tapeworm *Dipylidium caninum*

Heartworm *Dirofilaria immitis*

lariae circulate in the bloodstream, waiting to hitch a ride when the next mosquito bites. Once in the mosquito, the microfilariae develop into infective larvae and the entire process is repeated.

When dogs get infected with heartworm, over time they tend to develop symptoms associated with heart disease, such as coughing, exercise intolerance and potentially many other manifestations. Diagnosis is confirmed by either seeing the microfilariae themselves in blood samples or using immunologic tests (antigen testing) to identify the presence of adult heartworms. Since antigen tests measure the presence of adult heartworms and microfilarial tests measure offspring produced by adults, neither are positive until six to seven months after the initial infection. However, the beginning of damage can occur by fifth-stage larvae as early as three months after infection. Thus it is possible for dogs to be harboring problem-causing larvae for up to three months before either type of test would identify an infection.

The good news is that there are great protocols available for preventing heartworm in dogs. Testing is critical in the process, and it is important to understand the benefits as well as the limitations of such testing. All dogs six months of age or older that have not been on continuous heartworm-preventive medication should be

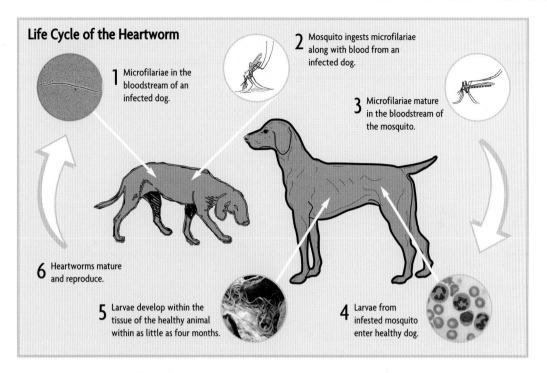

Life Cycle of the Heartworm

1 Microfilariae in the bloodstream of an infected dog.

2 Mosquito ingests microfilariae along with blood from an infected dog.

3 Microfilariae mature in the bloodstream of the mosquito.

4 Larvae from infested mosquito enter healthy dog.

5 Larvae develop within the tissue of the healthy animal within as little as four months.

6 Heartworms mature and reproduce.

screened with microfilarial or antigen tests. For dogs receiving preventive medication, periodic antigen testing helps assess the effectiveness of the preventives. The American Heartworm Society guidelines suggest that annual retesting may not be necessary when owners have absolutely provided continuous heartworm prevention. Retesting on a two- to three-year interval may be sufficient in these cases. However, your veterinarian will likely have specific guidelines under which heartworm preventives will be prescribed, and many prefer to err on the side of safety and retest annually.

It is indeed fortunate that heartworm is relatively easy to prevent, because treatments can be as life-threatening as the disease itself. Treatment requires a two-step process that kills the adult heartworms first and then the microfilariae. Prevention is obviously preferable; this involves a once-monthly oral or topical treatment. The most common oral preventives include ivermectin (not suitable for some breeds), moxidectin and milbemycin oxime; the once-a-month topical drug selamectin provides heartworm protection in addition to flea, tick and other parasite controls.

THE ABCs OF Emergency Care

Abrasions

Clean wound with running water or 3% hydrogen peroxide. Pat dry with gauze and spray with antibiotic. Do not cover.

Animal Bites

Clean area with soap and saline solution or water. Apply pressure to any bleeding area. Apply antibiotic ointment.

Antifreeze Poisoning

Induce vomiting and take dog to the vet.

Bee Sting

Remove stinger and apply soothing lotion or cold compress; give antihistamine in proper dosage.

Bleeding

Apply pressure directly to wound with gauze or towel for five to ten minutes. If wound does not stop bleeding, wrap wound with gauze and adhesive tape.

Bloat/Gastric Torsion

Immediately take the dog to the vet or emergency clinic; phone from car. No time to waste.

Burns

Chemical: Bathe dog with water and pet shampoo. Rinse in saline solution. Apply antibiotic ointment.

Acid: Rinse with water. Apply one part baking soda, two parts water to affected area.

Alkali: Rinse with water. Apply one part vinegar, four parts water to affected area.

Electrical: Apply antibiotic ointment. Seek veterinary assistance immediately.

Choking

If the dog is on the verge of collapsing, wedge a solid object, such as the handle of screwdriver, between molars on one side of the mouth to keep mouth open. Pull tongue out. Use long-nosed pliers or fingers to remove foreign object. Do not push the object down the dog's throat. For small or medium dogs, hold dog upside down by hind legs and shake firmly to dislodge foreign object.

Chlorine Ingestion

With clean water, rinse the mouth and eyes. Give the dog water to drink; contact the vet.

Constipation

Feed dog 2 tablespoons bran flakes with each meal. Encourage drinking water. Mix ¼ teaspoon mineral oil in dog's food.

Diarrhea

Withhold food for 12 to 24 hours. Feed dog anti-diarrheal with eyedropper. When feeding resumes, feed one part boiled hamburger, one part plain cooked rice, ¼ to ¾ cup four times daily.

Dog Bite

Snip away hair around puncture wound; clean with 3% hydrogen peroxide; apply tincture of iodine. If wound appears deep, take the dog to the vet.

Frostbite

Wrap the dog in a heavy blanket. Warm affected area with a warm bath for ten minutes. Red color to skin will return with circulation; if tissues are pale after 20 minutes, contact the vet.

Use a portable, durable container large enough to contain all items

Heat Stroke

Partially submerge the dog in cold water; if no response within ten minutes, contact the vet.

Hot Spots

Mix 2 packets Domeboro® with 2 cups water. Saturate cloth with mixture and apply to hot spots for 15 to 30 minutes. Apply antibiotic ointment. Repeat every six to eight hours.

Poisonous Plants

Wash affected area with soap and water. Cleanse with alcohol. For foxtail/grass, apply antibiotic ointment.

Rat Poison Ingestion

Induce vomiting. Keep dog calm, maintain dog's normal body temperature (use blanket or heating pad). Get to the vet for antidote.

Shock

Keep the dog calm and warm; call for veterinary assistance.

Snake Bite

If possible, bandage the area and apply pressure. If the area is not conducive to bandaging, use ice to control bleeding. Get immediate help from the vet.

Tick Removal

Apply flea and tick spray directly on tick. Wait one minute. Using tweezers or wearing plastic gloves, apply constant pull while grasping tick's body. Apply antibiotic ointment.

Vomiting

Restrict dog's water intake; offer a few ice cubes. Withhold food for next meal. Contact vet if vomiting persists longer than 24 hours.

DOG OWNER'S FIRST-AID KIT

❑ **Gauze bandages/swabs**
❑ **Adhesive and non-adhesive bandages**
❑ **Antibiotic powder**
❑ **Antiseptic wash**
❑ **Hydrogen peroxide 3%**
❑ **Antibiotic ointment**
❑ **Lubricating jelly**
❑ **Rectal thermometer**
❑ **Nylon muzzle**
❑ **Scissors and forceps**
❑ **Eyedropper**
❑ **Syringe**
❑ **Anti-bacterial/fungal solution**
❑ **Saline solution**
❑ **Antihistamine**
❑ **Cotton balls**
❑ **Nail clippers**
❑ **Screwdriver/pen knife**
❑ **Flashlight**
❑ **Emergency phone numbers**

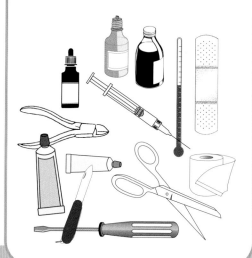

Is dog showing in your blood? Are you excited by the idea of gaiting your handsome Bull Terrier around the ring to the thunderous applause of an enthusiastic audience? Are you certain that your beloved Bull Terrier is flawless? You are not alone! Every loving owner thinks that his dog has no faults, or too few to mention. No matter how many times an owner reads the breed standard, he cannot find any faults in his aristocratic companion dog. If this sounds like you, and if you are considering entering your Bull Terrier in a dog show, here are some basic questions to ask yourself:

- Did you purchase a "show-quality" puppy from the breeder?
- Is your puppy at least six months of age?
- Does the puppy exhibit correct show type for his breed?
- Does your puppy have any disqualifying faults?
- Is your Bull Terrier registered with the American Kennel Club?
- How much time do you have to devote to training, grooming, conditioning and exhibiting your dog?
- Do you understand the rules and regulations of a dog show?
- Do you have time to learn how to show your dog properly?
- Do you have the financial resources to invest in showing your dog?
- Will you show the dog yourself or hire a professional handler?
- Do you have a vehicle that can accommodate your weekend trips to the dog shows?

Success in the show ring requires more than a pretty face, a waggy tail and a pocketful of liver. Even though dog shows can be exciting and enjoyable, the sport of conformation makes great demands on the exhibitors and the dogs. Winning exhibitors live for their dogs, devoting time and money to their dogs' presentation, conditioning and training. Very few novices, even those with good dogs, will find themselves in the winners' circle, though it does happen. Don't be disheartened, though. Every exhibitor began as a novice and worked his way up to the Group ring. It's the "working your way up" part that you must keep in mind.

AKC GROUPS

For showing purposes, the American Kennel Club divides its recognized breeds into seven groups: Terriers, Sporting Dogs, Hounds, Working Dogs, Toys, Non-Sporting Dogs and Herding Dogs.

Assuming that you have purchased a puppy of the correct type and quality for showing, let's begin to examine the world of showing and what's required to get started. Although the entry fee into a dog show is nominal, there are lots of other hidden costs involved with "finishing" your Bull Terrier, that is, making him a champion. Things like equipment, travel, training and conditioning all cost money. A more serious campaign will include fees for a professional handler, boarding, cross-country travel and advertising. Top-winning show dogs can represent a very considerable investment—over $100,000 has been spent in campaigning some dogs. (The investment can be less, of course, for owners who don't use professional handlers.)

Many owners, on the other hand, enter their "average" Bull Terriers in dog shows for the fun and enjoyment of it. Dog showing makes an absorbing hobby, with many rewards for dogs and owners alike. If you're having fun, meeting other people who share your interests and enjoying the overall experience, you likely will catch the "bug." Once the dog-show bug bites, its effects can last a lifetime; it's certainly much better than a deer tick! Soon you will be envisioning yourself in the center ring at the Westminster Kennel Club Dog Show in New York City, competing for the prestigious Best in Show cup. This magical dog show is televised annually from Madison Square Garden, and the victorious dog becomes a celebrity overnight.

AKC CONFORMATION SHOWING

GETTING STARTED

Visiting a dog show as a spectator is a great place to start. Pick up the show catalog to find out what time your

SHOW POTENTIAL

How possible is it to predict how your ten-week-old puppy will eventually do in the show ring? Most show dogs reach their prime at around three years of age, when their bodies are physically mature. Experienced breeders, having watched countless pups grow into Best of Breed winners, recognize the glowing attributes that spell "show potential." When selecting a puppy for show, it's best to trust the breeder to recommend which puppy will best suit your aspirations. Some breeders recommend starting with a male puppy, which likely will be more "typey" than his female counterpart.

breed is being shown, who is judging the breed and in which ring the classes will be held. To start, Bull Terriers compete against other Bull Terriers, and the winner is selected as Best of Breed by the judge. This is the procedure for each breed. At a group show, all of the Best of Breed winners go on to compete for Group One in their respective group. For example, all Best of Breed winners in a given group compete against each other; this is done for all seven groups. Finally, all seven group winners go head to head in the ring for the Best in Show award.

What most spectators don't understand is the basic idea of conformation. A dog show is often referred as a "conformation" show. This means that the judge should decide how each dog stacks up (conforms) to the breed standard for his given breed: how well does this Bull Terrier conform to the ideal representative detailed in the standard? Ideally, this is what happens. In reality, however, this ideal often gets slighted as the judge compares Bull Terrier #1 to Bull Terrier #2. Again, the ideal is that each dog is judged based on his merits in comparison to his breed standard, not in comparison to the other dogs in the ring. It is easier for judges to compare dogs of the same breed to decide which they think is the better specimen; in the Group and Best in Show ring,

however, it is very difficult to compare one breed to another, like apples to oranges. Thus the dog's conformation to the breed standard—not to mention advertising dollars and good handling—is essential to success in conformation shows. The dog described in the standard (the standard for each AKC breed is written and approved by the breed's national parent club and then submitted to the AKC for approval) is the perfect dog of that breed, and breeders keep their eye on the standard when they choose which dogs to breed, hoping to get

closer and closer to the ideal with each litter.

Another good first step for the novice is to join a dog club. You will be astonished by the many and different kinds of dog clubs in the country, with about 5,000 clubs holding events every year. Most clubs require that prospective new members present two letters of recommendation from existing members. Perhaps you've made some friends visiting a show held by a particular club and you would like to join that club. Dog clubs may specialize in a single breed, like a local or regional Bull Terrier club, or

Winning at a show in Holland, these two Bull Terriers were awarded Best Bitch and Reserve Best Bitch.

in a specific pursuit, such as obedience, tracking or hunting tests. There are all-breed clubs for all dog enthusiasts; they sponsor special training days, seminars on topics like grooming or handling or lectures on breeding or canine genetics. There are also clubs that specialize in certain types of dogs, like herding dogs, hunting dogs, companion dogs, etc.

A parent club is the national organization, sanctioned by the AKC, which promotes and safeguards its breed in the country. The Bull Terrier Club of America can be contacted on the Internet at www.btca.com. The parent club holds an annual national specialty show, usually in a different city each year, in which many of the country's top dogs, handlers and breeders gather to compete. At a specialty show, only members of a single breed are invited to participate. There are also group specialties, in which all members of a group are invited. For more information about dog clubs in your area, contact the AKC at www.akc.org on the Internet or write them at their Raleigh, NC address.

HOW SHOWS ARE ORGANIZED

Three kinds of conformation shows are offered by the AKC. There is the all-breed show, in which all AKC-recognized breeds can compete; the specialty show, which is for one breed only and usually sponsored by the breed's parent club and the group show, for all breeds in one of the AKC's seven groups. The Bull Terrier competes in the Terrier Group.

For a dog to become an AKC champion of record, the dog must earn 15 points at shows. The points must be awarded by at least three different judges and must include two "majors" under different judges. A "major" is a three-, four- or five-point win, and the number of points per win is determined by the number of dogs competing in the show on that day. (Dogs that are absent or are excused are not counted.) The number of points that are awarded varies from breed to breed. More dogs are needed to attain a major in more popular breeds, and fewer dogs are needed

EXPRESS YOURSELF
The most intangible of all canine attributes, expression speaks to the character of the breed, attained by the combined features of the head. The shape and balance of the dog's skull, the color and position of the eyes and the size and carriage of the head mingle to produce the correct expression of the breed. A judge may approach a dog and determine instantly whether the dog's face portrays the desired impression for the breed, conveying nobility, intelligence and alertness among other specifics of the breed standard.

in less popular breeds. Yearly, the AKC evaluates the number of dogs in competition in each division (there are 14 divisions in all, based on geography) and may or may not change the numbers of dogs required for each number of points. For example, a major in Division 2 (Delaware, New Jersey and Pennsylvania) recently required 17 dogs or 16 bitches for a three-point major, 29 dogs or 27 bitches for a four-point major and 51 dogs or 46 bitches for a five-point major. The Bull Terrier attracts numerically proportionate representation at all-breed shows.

Only one dog and one bitch of each breed can win points at a given show. There are no "co-ed" classes except for champions of record. Dogs and bitches do not compete against each other until they are champions. Dogs that are not champions (referred to as "class dogs") compete in one of five classes. The class in which a dog is entered depends on age and previous show wins. First there is the Puppy Class (sometimes divided further into classes for 6- to 9-month-olds and 9- to 12-month-olds); next is the Novice Class (for dogs that have no points toward their championship and whose only first-place wins have come in the Puppy Class or the Novice Class, the latter class limited to three first places); then there is the American-bred Class (for dogs bred in the US); the

Bred-by-Exhibitor Class (for dogs handled by their breeders or by immediate family members of their breeders) and the Open Class (for any non-champions). Any dog may enter the Open Class, regardless of age or win history, but to be

FOR MORE INFORMATION....

For reliable up-to-date information about registration, dog shows and other canine competitions, contact one of the national registries by mail or via the Internet.

American Kennel Club
5580 Centerview Dr., Raleigh, NC 27606-3390
www.akc.org

United Kennel Club
100 E. Kilgore Road, Kalamazoo, MI 49002
www.ukcdogs.com

Canadian Kennel Club
89 Skyway Ave., Suite 100, Etobicoke, Ontario
M9W 6R4, Canada
www.ckc.ca

The Kennel Club
1-5 Clarges St., Piccadilly, London W1Y 8AB, UK
www.the-kennel-club.org.uk

competitive the dog should be older and have ring experience.

The judge at the show begins judging the male dogs in the Puppy Class(es) and proceeds through the other classes. The judge awards first through fourth place in each class. The first-place winners of each class then compete with one another in the Winners Class to determine Winners Dog. The judge then starts over with the bitches, beginning with the Puppy Class(es) and proceeding up to the Winners Class to award Winners Bitch, just as he did with the dogs. A Reserve Winners Dog and Reserve Winners Bitch are also selected; they could be awarded the points in the case of a disqualification.

The Winners Dog and Winners Bitch are the two that are awarded the points for their breed. They then go on to compete with any champions of record (often called "specials") of their breed that are entered in the show. The champions may be dogs or bitches; in this class, all are shown together. The judge reviews the Winners Dog and Winners Bitch along with all of the champions to select the Best of Breed winner. The Best of Winners is selected between the Winners Dog and Winners Bitch; if one of these two is selected Best of Breed as well, he or she is automatically determined Best of Winners. Lastly, the judge selects Best of Opposite Sex to the Best of Breed winner. The Best of

Breed winner then goes on to the group competition.

At a group or all-breed show, the Best of Breed winners from each breed are divided into their respective groups to compete against one another for Group One through Group Four. Group One (first place) is awarded to the dog that best lives up to the ideal for his breed as described in the standard. A group judge, therefore, must have a thorough working knowledge of many breed standards. After placements have been made in each group, the seven Group One winners (from the Sporting Group, Toy Group, Hound Group, etc.) compete against each other for the top honor, Best in Show.

There are different ways to find out about dog shows in your area. The American Kennel Club's monthly magazine, the *American Kennel Gazette* is accompanied by, the *Events Calendar*; this magazine is available through subscription. You can also look on the AKC's and your parent club's websites for information and check the event listings in your local newspaper.

Your Bull Terrier must be six months of age or older and registered with the AKC in order to be entered in AKC-sanctioned shows in which there are classes for the Bull Terrier. Your Bull Terrier also must not possess any disqualifying faults and must be sexually intact. The reason for the latter is simple: dog shows are the proving grounds to determine which dogs and bitches are worthy of being bred. If they cannot be bred, that defeats the purpose! On that note, only dogs that have achieved championships, thus proving their excellent quality, should be bred. If you have spayed or neutered your dog, however, there are many AKC events other than conformation, such as obedience trials, agility trials and the Canine Good Citizen® program, in which you and your Bull Terrier can participate.

OBEDIENCE TRIALS

Mrs. Helen Whitehouse Walker, a Standard Poodle fancier, can be credited with introducing obedience trials to the United States. In the 1930s, she designed a series of exercises based on those of the Associated Sheep, Police, Army Dog Society of Great Britain. These exercises were intended to evaluate the working relationship between dog and owner. Since those early days of the sport in the US, obedience trials have grown more and more popular, and now more than 2,000 trials each year attract over 100,000 dogs and their owners. Any dog registered with the AKC, regardless of neutering or other disqualifications that would preclude entry in conformation competition, can participate in obedience trials.

There are three levels of difficulty in obedience competition. The first (and easiest) level is

You don't have to be an expert to get started in showing your Bull Terrier. Should you have an interest and a show-quality dog, contact your local breed or kennel club to find out about activities in which you can gain experience.

the Novice, in which dogs can earn the Companion Dog (CD) title. The intermediate level is the Open level, in which the Companion Dog Excellent (CDX) title is awarded. The advanced level is the Utility level, in which dogs compete for the Utility Dog (UD) title. Classes at each level are further divided into "A" and "B," with "A" for beginners and "B" for those with more experience. In order to win a title at a given level, a dog must earn three "legs." A "leg" is accomplished when a dog scores 170 or higher (200 is a perfect score). The scoring system gets a little trickier when you understand that a dog must score more than 50% of the points available for each exercise in order to actually earn the points. Available points for each exercise range between 20 and 40.

Once he's earned the UD title, a dog can go on to win the prestigious title of Utility Dog Excellent (UDX) by winning "legs" in ten shows. Additionally, Utility Dogs who win

Up, up and away—a Bully doing his thing at an agility trial!

obedience or in the top three for his breed in obedience. The title at stake here is that of National Obedience Champion (NOC).

AGILITY TRIALS

Agility trials became sanctioned by the AKC in August 1994, when the first licensed agility trials were held. Since that time, agility certainly has grown in popularity by leaps and bounds, literally! The AKC allows all registered breeds (including Miscellaneous Class breeds) to participate, providing the dog is 12 months of age or older. Agility is designed so that the handler demonstrates how well the dog can work at his side. The handler directs

"legs" in Open B and Utility B earn points toward the lofty title of Obedience Trial Champion (OTCh.). Established in 1977 by the AKC, this title requires a dog to earn 100 points as well as three first places in a combination of Open B and Utility B classes under three different judges. The "brass ring" of obedience competition is the AKC's National Obedience Invitational. This is an exclusive competition for only the cream of the obedience crop. In order to qualify for the invitational, a dog must be ranked in either the top 25 all-breeds in

MEET THE AKC

The American Kennel Club is the main governing body of the dog sport in the United States. Founded in 1884, the AKC consists of 500 or more independent dog clubs plus 4,500 affiliated clubs, all of which follow the AKC rules and regulations. Additionally, the AKC maintains a registry for pure-bred dogs in the US and works to preserve the integrity of the sport and its continuation in the country. Over 1,000,000 dogs are registered each year, representing about 150 recognized breeds. There are over 15,000 competitive events held annually for which over 2,000,000 dogs enter to participate. Dogs compete to earn over 40 different titles, from champion to Companion Dog to Master Agility Champion.

his dog through, over, under and around an obstacle course that includes jumps, tires, the dog walk, weave poles, pipe tunnels, collapsed tunnels and more. While working his way through the course, the dog must keep one eye and ear on the handler and the rest of his body on the course. The handler runs along with the dog, giving verbal and hand signals to guide the dog through the course.

    The first organization to promote agility trials in the US was the United States Dog Agility Association, Inc. (USDAA). Established in 1986, the USDAA sparked the formation of many member clubs around the country. To participate in USDAA trials, dogs must be at least 18 months of age. The USDAA and AKC both offer titles to winning dogs, although the exercises and requirements of the two organizations differ.

    Agility trials are a great way to keep your dog active, and they will keep you running, too! You should join a local agility club to learn more about the sport. These clubs offer sessions in which you can introduce your dog to the various obstacles as well as training classes to prepare him for competition. In no time, your dog will be climbing A-frames, crossing the dog walk and flying over hurdles, all with you right beside him. Your heart will leap every time your dog jumps through the hoop—and you'll be having just as much (if not more) fun!

TRACKING

Tracking tests are exciting ways to test your Bull Terrier's instinctive scenting ability on a competitive level. All dogs have a nose, and all breeds are welcome in tracking tests. The first AKC-licensed tracking test took place in 1937 as part of the Utility level at an obedience trial, and thus competitive tracking was officially begun. The first title, Tracking Dog (TD), was offered in 1947, ten years after the first official tracking test. It was not until 1980 that the AKC added the title Tracking Dog Excellent (TDX), which was followed by the title Versatile Surface Tracking (VST) in 1995. Champion Tracker (CT) is awarded to a dog who has earned all three of those titles.

The talents of the Bull Terrier know no bounds. Training your Bull Terrier for agility trials exercises both you and the dog. An active Bull Terrier is a happy one!

INDEX

My Bull Terrier

PUT YOUR PUPPY'S FIRST PICTURE HERE

Dog's Name _____

Date _____ Photographer _____